HEROIN

OUT OF THE ASHES

T.A. BECHEL

T.A. Bechel Fiction
Alton, IL 62002

For More info, visit: TABechel.com

ISBN-13: 978-1725195653

ISBN-10: 1725195658

BECAUSE WE ONLY USE
THE BEST

An essay:
Hell and Salvation in the Here and Now

What do I want to do with my life?

No matter where I am, or what I've accomplished that is always the one question I cannot stop asking myself.

After deciding to start over, leaving the pain and the ugliness of my previous book in the rear-view mirror, I enrolled back in college, where a class professor told me, "Go forthright in your discoveries."

I wasn't exactly sure what he meant at first. When I received his e-mail, I looked up 'forthright' in the dictionary and came to understand what he was trying to tell me - to go forthright in my discoveries I would have to continue to move forward in my life, allowing myself to remain honest and authentic.

Honesty is hard for many of us; all of us lie at some point in our lives. Sometimes, the mistruths are spoken by design, while other times it is pure impulse. When I was in active addiction, my instincts went haywire, and my survival mode was definitely out of whack, caught in a web of lies.

Alcohol. Drugs. Fast food. Not really the prime combination for a body to function at its full potential. I felt in active addiction that my potential was to hurt those around me. I find it interesting that when someone does harm to us, and our feelings get hurt, we chastise the perpetrator. On the other hand, when we hurt someone and get scolded, we try to justify our actions. Whether you are a believer in a God or not, the Lord's Prayer says, *"Forgive me my trespasses, as I forgive those who trespass against me."* It is sometimes hard to forgive those that have hurt us. More often, it is difficult to forgive ourselves when we hurt those around us. Selfishness and self-centeredness are components of human nature that can easily slip from our grasp if we are not aware of our desires.

"The road to Hell is paved with good intentions" *(ancient proverb thought to have originated with Saint Bernard of Clairvaux).*

Regardless of its origin, this makes perfect sense to me. I must learn to take a moment, or even a series of moments, to reflect and ask myself what my motivations and intentions truly are. Putting forth action must come next. When I realized I had hurt someone, I had to do my best to figure out why and correct it.

The path of destruction I left in the wake of my active addiction was thick with guilt and shame. The anchors that prevented me from sailing freely had to be lifted. I had to find a way to cut the ties to these self-defeating weights and realize that the chains I shackled myself with could be successfully removed for good.

Hell seems to be something we experience while living, not after death. My daily torment, combined with the thought of evaporating out of existence, was a deadly cocktail that I didn't want to drink any longer. The change wasn't going to take place by just removing the drugs and alcohol from my life. The change had to be initiated. Then, once the process had begun, I would have

4

to welcome change into life just as I had a force increasingly larger than myself - God. I invited Him into my heart with an invitation written in my cries of sorrow, and He RSVP'd when my desperation became too heavy a burden to carry alone.

I was granted true freedom the day I fell to my knees and begged for an escape.

I was no longer looking through a kaleidoscope and trying to make sense of a distorted reality. My perception became my reality, and my reality became my Hell; I was shown salvation and understanding.

This is the story of that journey.

WARNING

For those in active addiction or early recovery from drug and alcohol addiction, there are graphic details recounting drug/alcohol use in descriptive detail. These may serve as triggers for some.

Foreword – Yin and Yang

The past can sometimes be made up of distorted memories that we bend to our self-justification in an attempt to tolerate where we are in the present moment.

Some of us pick up blame and hate. Some of us hold onto what we want as moments that can define, shape, and mold us. Some of us learn from it...some of us don't. I believe a majority of us would love to have a past empty of regrets, trauma, deceit, lies, and selfishness.

Though, as strange as this may sound, some of us thrive on chaos; it's what we come to know as comfortable. Our scarred past is used as a blanket of dark matter to permeate misery. Some of us welcome it with open arms, only to poison those around us as we laugh and gallop with sickening joy. Philosopher, poet, and novelist George Santayana said, "Those who cannot remember the past are condemned to repeat it."

As I sat there, arm around Christina and our son's head lying on her lap as he napped, I couldn't help but remember a darker and more frightening time. See, the grittiness and chaos I experienced was nearly my downfall. Today is a different story; I live every moment more cautiously and aware, reminding myself each morning what I was like, what change took place, and what my life is like today.

This *normal* life with my family that I love so much today can change in the blink of an eye. One poor decision could crack open a vat of depression, madness, and internal carnage, experienced so vividly when I was dragged around by a master that wanted to see me slowly suffer through torture, isolation, and self-hate.

Only a short time ago (or maybe a lifetime), I was 165 pounds, my DC shoes had matching holes with my baggy jeans, unwashed for more than two weeks. The memory *shot* through my frontal lobe, causing a daze of familiar feelings that I NEVER want to forget. As Santayana points out, I can repeat the past if I forget.

I don't ever want to forget.

This flashback reminded me that my future once looked bleak, and I was lost in an abyss of absolute terror. The obsession of falsified comfort of a love affair that ends only in deceit and betrayal for most of us invaded my mind as I walked the streets. I shuffled, sun beating down on my face, as I fought the internal battle of wanting to use.

I didn't want to use. I didn't have any money. I felt I didn't have anyone. I abandoned God. I walked, passing house after house. It was all a glimpse into a reality from which I felt totally distant. I was an outsider. I was a leper. I was a disgrace. I might as well be an extraterrestrial from a distant universe.

Thoughts of using wouldn't leave. Thoughts of going to the gas station to take some woman's purse just to get off this sickness carousel hammered away. I was battling my diseased self. I was fighting my thoughts. Suicide was an option. The daily torment was the same, day in and day out. The flame infested labyrinth of Hell covered me. I was disconnected from love and support. And my puppy-dog love for heroin showed its true colors. It was a covert enemy posing as a friend. It was an informant for Satan himself. His foot soldier befriended me.

This love and lust for heroin and other drugs did precisely what they were set out to do - claim another victim of what some call circumstance. It made me crazy and unlovable. It was slowly strangling me. It was like I was in an invisible pool of quicksand, knowing death was imminent. In a situation like this, I think many of us begin to welcome death. We invite that specter known as Death, sickle and all, as a house guest of our flimsy faith...and anything good evaporates.

And then I am back. The warmth of Christina's body, the feeling of her lungs inflating and deflating, and our son resting comfortably on her lap, was almost paradoxical.

I wasn't supposed to make it out alive. I was supposed to become a statistic and succumb to the grip of *Satan* and his assassins. Addiction should have been the victor.

This reminder, this trip down the yellow brick road, in the comfort of our now stable home was needed. Evil was abolished. A spiritual vortex sucked me up and saved me from a reality that is familiar to many.

Too many.

Chapter 1
Birth of a Recovering Addict

I stared out the window and watched the open fields pass by. I had spent most of my time growing up in the city, so when I saw farm equipment quietly sitting in a field, I was not only intrigued but curious how it all worked. I am not sure if you are anything like me, but when I spend a lengthy amount of time in a car, I begin to study everything that passes.

The last fifteen minutes of the ride to the sober living home was filled with comfortable silence. Melted into the passenger seat, I didn't feel the need to talk; maybe because up until then, I had talked the ear off the gentleman kind enough to drive me to the facility.

In all honesty, I felt for once in my life that sitting in silence, lost in my thoughts, was okay. Before that ride, I was never able to sit in a room without noise...especially if someone was in the room with me. I always felt the need to fill the silence with conversation, no matter how meaningless.

And I realized...I missed Christina and my daughters, and I hadn't even been gone for two hours.

After a two-hour trip north, and a few more curves on the road, we approached the city housing the sober living home. On the edge of the road, a few feet before entering the city limits, stood a sign inscribed with the town name and population.

The population was 600.

Only 600! I thought to myself.

I chuckled slightly and developed doubts, but I knew I had to stay and get well.

As we pulled into the gravel parking lot, I could hear the rocks crunch beneath the tires of the car. My heart started racing because I knew the driver was soon going to leave. Leave me behind.

I knew I could get along with most new people I meet, but the idea of spending a minimum of six months with them almost made me vomit. Six months of dealing with other people's bullshit on top of mine. People that were just as sick as me.

I had been to a couple of 28-day treatment facilities before, so I knew that there would be drama – the kind that comes with people trying to discover themselves. I would soon learn that staying on my side of the street and not worrying about other people's baggage would benefit not only me but my family, as well.

It was a strange feeling, being in the moment as I was getting out of the car. My senses were heightened, which was new to me because there were no drugs or alcohol in my system to falsify them as there had been for so many years. The click of the car door when I pulled the handle back to open it sounded louder than it probably was. The mild popping noise the rocks made underneath the rubber soles of my shoes helped create a moment almost surreal. I took a deep breath and looked at the building.

It was an old, two-story schoolhouse encased in red bricks with some of the mortar missing here and there between them. The front of the building was damaged in a storm, and a whole chunk of bricks was gone, exposing the second layer of the structure.

This building looks the way I feel inside – broken. Then a warm feeling came over me. Everything was going to be okay. It was entirely reasonable to fear the unknown. That's what life is, right? When breaking down the scheme of things, it is a series of moments that we desperately do our best to control, but ultimately can only strive to survive. Throughout the centuries, leaders have used a type of fearmongering to penetrate our minds to achieve their distorted agendas, trying to convince the masses that we need them.

I was beginning to realize that God, the Creator, a higher power, the Great Spirit, and the power of consciousness was everywhere and accessible to everyone. I didn't have to be afraid any longer.

I put the strap of my duffle bag around my shoulder and walked toward the back of the building, following the driver to my new, albeit temporary, home.

With his hands in each of his front pockets, he asked, "You ready?"

I grinned.

"Well, I have to be. I don't really have too many options if I want to live."

I wasn't referring to the drugs and alcohol that were slowly killing me. I knew that my life couldn't be ransacked daily with fear of powerful people in the world that commit monstrous atrocities, along with the other things that frightened me. I knew that I was becoming something I feared the most – a monster under someone's bed. It was apparent that a positive change was needed for my survival.

It seems almost fitting that every single one of us could become something we don't want to be. I didn't plan on becoming a heroin junkie, but I did. I was scared, worried, and completely clueless how I should live my life, but a presence was with me that offered the assurance that I was going to be okay.

My friend and I walked to the back door of the building. He grabbed the handle and swung the door open. The staircase leading to the sober living home's office looked like a mile-long climb...it was only about ten steps.

If we don't take the first step, then we cannot take the second.

My heart pounded. I took one final breath and the first step forward. My foot crossed the threshold of the building, and I was now fully committed.

When the student is ready, the teacher will appear.

I was ready.

Chapter 2
A World without Hangers and a Ten-Minute Phone Call

I stepped through the office door and felt like I was moving in slow motion.

My eyes wandered the room, taking in all of my surroundings. I noticed the computer and phone station that sat directly to my right. A tall bookshelf housed recovery books and what looked like an old first aid kit. A lone coffee pot sat on a table with all the extras you add to coffee to make the taste tolerable. I noticed two metal file cabinets – they could have been tan or black - standing side-by-side. There was a table shoved in the corner, cluttered with miscellaneous things like posters and unmarked boxes.

A lady wearing prescription glasses with short brown hair set down her pen and greeted us. She extended her hand and introduced herself.

"Hi, you must be Ty. My name is Sally."

"Hello, Sally. What did I get myself into?"

Her smile was welcoming and eased some of the tension that I was feeling.

"Well, I asked myself the same thing when I got here, but trust me, you *will* get well. It's a great place to be."

I assumed by her statement that she was also a resident at the sober living home, or had been at one point in time.

I sat my duffel bag down on the floor. Sally walked to one of the file cabinets and pulled out a cup and little square package. I had been part of the treatment world long enough to know she had an instant drug test for me to take. My friend sat down at a ten-foot-long, cherry red conference table as I headed to the bathroom. It was an aggravating feeling knowing that people couldn't just automatically trust me.

I obliged them without any attitude. After all, I had to remember-I did *fake* and *time* my drug tests in the past.

If you want to gain trust, you must first become trustworthy.

I'd spent the past four or five years always living in survival mode. I was hunting and gathering drugs, alcohol, attention, women, and anything else to make me feel better. I was chasing them to survive. My brain had been changed, and in the coming months, I would work on repairing some of the damage I had caused the most important organ in my body.

Next, I could work on my relationships—the ones that once had a natural trust but were now nearly completely eroded. It was an odd feeling, thinking about how others perceived me in my addiction. I stood there and pissed in that cup so that my life could get better. I was ready to get over the uncomfortable and jagged feelings I had felt for so long.

And I was ready to stop having to piss for people.

The home's director had a wiry, white beard and stood about five-feet-two. He had a toothpick hanging out of his mouth as he reached out his hand to introduce himself.

"Hi, Ty is it?" he asked, shaking my hand.

He seemed welcoming, and I didn't feel any negative vibes, so I warmly accepted him.

"Yes, sir. What's your name?"

He tossed the toothpick into the nearest wastebasket.

"My name is Roger. What's your drug of choice?"

I was so tired of answering that question, mostly because *everything* was pretty much my drug of choice. The only drugs that I hadn't ingested, snorted, or blasted into my veins were hallucinogens (only because I didn't want to have a bad trip, despite what Timothy Leary said) and methamphetamines. My brain was always thinking, and I pictured myself removing my own eyeballs if I tried expanding that mind.

"Well, my drug of choice is almost everything, but the last few years it was any opiate, mainly heroin," I said.

Roger had a peculiar way of answering questions by nodding and muttering what I think was the word "okay." It actually could have been "mmkay." Regardless, gauging him the first time I met him was hard. I couldn't tell if he liked me, or didn't, or if he thought I was a piece of shit or someone that needed help.

As an addict in active addiction, we always size people up when we meet them. It is probably some acquired survival instinct that evolves after you've spent a few years *ripping and running*. You try to figure out from the outside if each new person means you harm. As an addict, you don't trust many people. You don't even trust yourself. I think it's because of the dangerous situations we put ourselves in and, along with the stigma and disdain addicts receive, we are always on the defensive.

Sally asked if I wanted to smoke before she showed me to my room.

I needed a cigarette.

Standing outside the entrance doors, *hotboxing* my first cigarette in three hours, I looked around the yard. A fire pit sat a few feet in front of me, and there was a garden of mostly tomato plants nearby. In the distance, there was a house standing alone near an open field. I was definitely in farm country.

My dad and I used to garden together – pulling weeds was my job – and it was one of the few times we bonded when I was younger. The memory brought me a sense of peace.

As I stubbed out the cigarette, a resident came around the corner of the building, startling me.

"Hi," she said, her own cigarette hanging out of her mouth.

I took her inventory instantly. She seemed okay. She'd taken the time to say hello, and that was cool of her.

"What's up," I said with a grin. "My name's Ty. Who are you?"

Her laugh was rough, but she smiled.

"My name is Sandy. So, first day, huh. What was your drug of choice?"

Son of a...

"H," I answered in street slang. "Really anything, but H was my favorite."

I had to uphold an image with people with which I had the most in common. I was still trying to be the cool guy. I was trying to get away from something that I wasn't, but getting completely comfortable in my skin wouldn't happen for a while.

But I was pretty excited to be at the sober living home, and I think Sandy could sense my exuberance.

She smiled sarcastically.

"Why are you so chipper?"

I wasn't sure if I should express what I felt – excited, happy, and free. I didn't want Sandy to think I was a square or some type of snitch, but for some reason, I put it all out there.

"I am ready for a change. The drugs and the life I was living were destroying me. I'm out of jail and never wanna go back...ever."

I was on a pink cloud. I was ready to take on the world and accept my position in life.

Sandy cocked her head in confusion.

"I wish I was that happy to be here."

I smiled.

"It was great meeting you. I gotta get with Sally for a few things and get my room together."

She put out her cigarette and just laughed. "Yeah, good to meet you."

When I made my way back to the office, Sally was waiting for me. I grabbed my duffle bag and followed her up two flights of stairs to a closet full of hygiene products and bedding.

"Alright, let's see here," she said, handing me plain white sheets and a comforter with bears and trees on it. Bears. And trees.

I think she could read my mind, or it was the look of disgust and worry on my face. I couldn't help but think of everyone who might have slept with these linens and comforter before me.

She put her hand on top of the comforter and looked me in the eyes. "I assure you, Ty, we wash these. Things will be okay."

As much as I tried to hold my composure and smile, I guess the nervousness was apparent. Standing in the closet full of personal care necessities made it real, and I started feeling sorry for myself. I thought of my daughters and Christina.

Sally's words helped ease the onset of anxiety. Encouraging words helped so much in my early days of recovery.

We stepped out of the closet, and she paused to lock it before leading me to my new bedroom. The room I'd be living out of was long and narrow. The drywall was peeling in some spots, and there was a gap roughly a foot wide between the top of the interior wall and the ceiling —everything I said could be heard in the next bedroom over. If they really wanted, they could even look over into my room.

Privacy would not be an option, but at least there was a window (even if it only looked out over the parking area). I didn't like the room at all; it reminded me of the squalor I thought I lived in with my mom back in high school.

I had to mentally prepare myself for what was to come. There are a lot of ups and downs in early recovery, and I couldn't let my emotions get the best of me before I'd even gotten started. I sucked up the pity party that was entering my mind and told myself that this was better than jail or couch surfing.

Sally smiled and patted my shoulder to comfort me.

"I'll let you get settled in. Come on down to the office once you're all unpacked. We'll be having lunch soon,"

She left the room, and I stood alone, looking around like it was going to change if I stared at it long enough. I closed my eyes and prayed. "*Okay, God, I am not exactly certain of this place, but I know this is better than where I was headed.*"

I opened my eyes, took a deep breath, and unpacked. There was only one hanger in the armoire.

"What the fuck?" I shouted.

A knock on the door took my attention away from the seriously hanger-impaired piece of furniture.

"Hey, Ty is it?" asked what I assumed was another resident.

Great. I really wasn't in the mood for a receiving line.

"Sally asked me to bring you this dresser," he said. "You want me to bring it in now?"

I hadn't even noticed that there wasn't a dresser in the room. I guess I was distracted by everything else going on inside my head.

"Might as well, right?" I said with a forced smile.

"My name is Jimmy. Welcome. It's not that bad here."

Even though I wanted to be alone for the moment, it felt good that he'd taken the time to introduce himself and help bring me a dresser.

We sat the dresser near the foot of my twin sized bed, and I remembered how hanger-less I felt.

"What's a guy gotta do to get some hangers around here?"

For whatever reason, I was really pissed off that I didn't have any. It shouldn't have been that big of a deal, but I managed to make it into a doozie.

He scratched his arm and laughed. "Well, hangers are kinda scarce. I can give you a couple extra I got."

"Really?" I asked, unsure.

"You bet," he fired back over his shoulder without hesitation, and suddenly he was back with three hangers.

"Thanks, Jimmy. It means a lot."

"No problem, you joining us for lunch?"

I suddenly felt a little bit better. "Yeah, after I'm done here I will be down."

He left, and I stood there, still angry about the unfortunate hanger situation, but not nearly as psychotic as I had been. Four was better than one.

I hung up four shirts and accepted the fact I'd have to put the rest of my clothes in the dresser. *What am I, some kind of animal?*

For a guy that didn't have much, I was quite demanding.

After I put my belongings away and made my bed, I looked at the small desk in my bedroom. My first thought was that I wanted to start writing again. I felt a spark in my belly; I couldn't tell if it was hunger or the passion I so longed for since I was a child.

I made my way back to the office.

Sally took me downstairs to the lunchroom, which was actually much more like a cafeteria. I walked into the

23

brightly lit eating quarters, and a majority of the residents were sitting down, eating their lunch. I can't remember what we ate that day, but the awkward feeling of eating their food set in. Sally introduced me to everyone, and I sheepishly waved. The whole time I was preparing my lunch, it felt like everyone was staring at me. It was the same feeling I got as a child during my first day at a new school.

I sat a few seats down from everyone, feeling like an outsider. Remember, it is always hard to trust at first, so a room full of new people felt pretty intense. My friend and ride came down to the lunch room, easing a bit of tension, but only for a moment. He was coming to tell me goodbye. I shook his hand and thanked him for taking the time to bring me.

He left, and suddenly there I was, trapped in a new place with complete strangers, about to make the most significant change I could possibly make in my life.

Eventually, one of the other residents broke the ice, asking me a few mundane questions. It was just small talk, but it alleviated some of the social awkwardness I was experiencing.

From him, I learned that the residents prepared meals for one another and took care of their own laundry, among other things.

"What was that loud bell I heard earlier?" I asked Sandy, referring to the loud, obnoxious fire alarm that jolted me out of my thoughts earlier.

She told me it was the bell that alerts the whole house that it was time for either lunch or chores.

This is all so strange.

I was sort of in culture shock. I was taking everything in and trying to sort it all out. I had to go to recovery support meetings, house meetings, and even see a therapist once a week. I told myself I was going to make the best of it so I couldn't keep complaining when I was going to have shelter, food, and a positive support network.

Quit your bellyaching and embrace a fantastic opportunity.

I finished lunch, and one of the residents took me on a tour of the building. There was a basketball court – I loved basketball – and some weights.

I saw the laundry room and the food pantry. I liked the idea of the pantry; it reminded me of my uncle who died of a heart attack. He used to do a lot of volunteering with his church and Operation Blessing. I started to feel like things were going to work out. I knew I could give back to the society from which I had taken so much from.

It may not be the Peace Corps, but it was definitely a way to regain some self-worth.

When the mini-tour was over, I was able to call Christina (designated times for phone calls; ten minutes each, twice a day).

She answered the phone on the first ring.

"Hello, Ty?"

"Yeah, it's me," I replied, trying to not choke up on the phone.

"How are you?" she asked as her voice cracked and quivered with what I assumed was sadness.

I tried to hold it together, but the tears were welling up already

"I…I miss you guys. This is so weird."

I could hear her sniffling on the other end of the phone. She was trying to stop crying before she answered me.

She worked so hard not to show it when she was upset. I could picture her, biting her upper lip with the bottom row of her front teeth. It's a habit of hers to this day.

"Are you biting your lip?" I said, chuckling to try and make her feel just a little bit better.

"Yes, I am, asshole," she laughed. "I can't believe you're going to be gone for six months. Or longer."

I looked down at the floor, avoiding any residents that might view my crying as weakness.

"I know, but it's not bad here. A lot of change will have to take place. I have to cook for fifteen or sixteen other people living here."

"You like cooking, so that shouldn't be too bad," she reassured me.

Then I was reminded that rebuilding my choices' destruction reached beyond just my insecurities. Christina had her own, as well.

"You better stay away from girls while you're there!" she suddenly announced.

This was going to be hard; I missed my family, even though I knew I was no good at home right now. I kept using that *one* more time, which inevitably turned into binges. I was scared that drug court was fed up with me and frightened that Christina was going to leave me for someone else. Better looking. With a job. And no drug habit.

There were a lot of emotions crammed into those ten minutes.

The day flew by. In-house meeting. Dinner. Outside recovery meeting. I was able to meet a few people from that outside meeting that were very supportive of the sober living home.

Before I knew it, I was back in my room…a room so quiet I could hear a few of the other residents moving around in their spaces. It gave me time to unwind and think about everything. I laid on my back in the bed – both hands behind my head and my legs crossed – listening to the silence. I could hear the passing cars and the light wind brushing up against the window. I kicked off my shoes, closed my eyes, and prayed (more of a "talk" with God, I guess). I was thankful for being alive and asked for the guidance to get well.

Before I knew it, I'd dozed off into a peaceful sleep.

Chapter 3
A Hot Shower and Some Breakfast Commentary

When I woke up the following morning, I had to remind myself where I was. I wasn't at home...or in jail...or worse.

Waking up in an unfamiliar place proved an eerie reminder of late-night benders. I couldn't tell you how many times I awoke (came to) after a night of drinking in a strange and foreign place. The uncomfortable feeling faded as my head cleared and I remembered where I was.

I stretched my whole body. It felt good to be clean and sober; it felt even better because I was doing it consciously.

I couldn't help but wonder what Christina and the girls were doing, but I tried to distract myself. I got out of bed, gathered my clothes for the day, and left my room in search of an open shower. The first bathroom I went to had two showers that stood side-by-side. Even though you couldn't see the other guys showering, I still felt uncomfortable getting out of the shower into an open room with another shower. A floor below, the men's bathroom in the gym had a single shower, but the entrance didn't have a door. I decided to put a chair in front of the entrance in the hope that it would deter anyone else from coming in.

It was a surreal moment. It sounds silly, I know, but I was getting ready to take a shower somewhere other than home. Though I have showered at friend's houses, in jail, and at treatment centers many times, there is nothing quite like being in the security of your own home to sleep and bathe. As I turned on the water and tested the temperature, I looked down at the shower floor. I couldn't help but think of how many other feet were in the shower before me.

You would think to take a shower would be easily done, but I couldn't quit thinking of other people's ugly toes and the foot fungus community that could be living on that shower floor.

Stop being a wuss!

I stood there and laughed at my personal dilemma. "Fuck it," I said, and stepped into the steam-filled shower. The water felt amazing. As it flattened my hair and ran down my face, I closed my eyes and felt each bead of water run down my body. I stood there...naked...missing Christina...caressing my chest...

Sorry, this isn't going to turn into porn. It was just a regular, ordinary, everyday shower...except that the water felt more incredible than it had in a long time.

When I stepped out, a blast of cold air finished waking me up. My thoughts were a marathon as I grabbed my towel and began to dry off - I had stepped out of my life and into a new one filled with routines and rules. The change in extremes was noticeable and uncomfortable. But I also realized that change was possible and getting past the snafus was expected.

I returned to my room with my laundry, reassuring myself that I would be okay. I knew I had to stay positive to make it through the program and back home to Christina and the kids clean and sober.

I sat my clothes down in the basket. The room was quiet, and I wasn't sure who, if anyone, was in the other rooms. I could only hear my thoughts and the buzzing noise you get in your ear when silence has covered you like a blanket. *Wa-wa-wa-wa* was the sound that penetrated my ears.

And then the doubts arrived with rage and intensity. I started thinking of all the times I lost my temper with my daughters and what horrible things I put my oldest through. I felt like I was running away...a coward. I wasn't sure what a *man* was supposed to be, but I definitely didn't feel like one.

I could hear my family and friends. *He's a lost cause. He's never going to change. He'd probably be better off dead. Once a junkie, always a junkie. He's a fucking loser* (my personal favorite).

It was like a freeway had opened up in my head, and everyone was speeding and honking their horns. Guilt came quickly, wrapping itself around my neck. I had trouble breathing. My eyes swelled with tears. Dammit. I was so tired of crying, but I couldn't stop.

What have I done? Maybe they are right. Perhaps I should just give up.

All of the negatives that I heard over the past few years - in jail, family living rooms, and in my own home - were drowning me. The drugs were gone, but my taunting past was not. If you have dinner with the devil, there isn't much room for dessert. I thought I could never enjoy life. Worst of all, I didn't feel like I deserved that life.

I fell to my knees, buried my face in my hands, and wept.

Suddenly, as I sat on the floor with my knees bent and hands covered in salty tears, I was startled by that fucking bell. It was time for breakfast, and I didn't want anyone to see me like this. I dried my eyes with my towel and took a few deep breaths.

I made my bed – something I hadn't done in a long time – and went downstairs to get something to eat. I didn't think I was starving until the aroma of freshly cooked sausage hit me. I picked up a plate and a fork and slabbed a few sausage patties and scrambled eggs on my plate. I am not exactly sure why, but the steam resting comfortably above the eggs, vanishing in thin air, was satisfying.

I sat down at the table with the rest of the residents. No one was saying anything, but I guessed that was usual, being it was only eight in the morning. The scraping noise of silverware against plates filled the room.

One of the residents asked about my night. I wasn't in the mood to talk, but I didn't want to be rude.

"It was all right. I slept better than I thought I would."

He smiled.

"You know, your eyes look pretty puffy. Are you okay?"

Dammit. I thought to myself. *I don't know you. Don't try to lift my spirits.*

"I'm good. Miss my family a bit."

Another resident decided now was the time to offer his two cents.

"Hey, it's okay, dude. I think we have all cried here once or twice."

And with that, they were off and running. The people around me began talking about all of the times they had cried, but I just couldn't get engaged in the conversation. I looked down at the last few bites on my plate, then got up. I scraped off the remaining food, sat the plate in the dishwater, and headed back to my room for a few minutes before the morning house meeting.

If this is how I am going to feel every day, this is going to be one long stay.

Chapter 4
The Light Breaks Through

I managed to make it through my first week without any scrapes or bruises. I can't tell you how many times I cried at night, wondering what I would do with my life. But I was finally getting comfortable with the residents; I wasn't so guarded around them, and I started talking and joking around.

My first weekend away from my family was liberating and sad all at the same time - I wasn't in jail, but I was alone. When we were allowed to talk on the phone, I called Christina the first chance I had. I dialed her number, and the phone kept ringing; I was getting nervous she wasn't going to answer. Her voicemail picked up. I hung up the receiver and got up from the chair. Suddenly, the phone rang.

"Hello?"

All I could hear was the background noise of the radio playing and someone talking.

"Oh, hello, hi, is Ty there?" said the girl on the other end.

My worry that I wasn't going to be able to talk to Christina melted quickly once I heard her voice. It may not seem like such a monumental task, but the phone in that house was worth more than gold, and with sixteen other residents, it could get quite chaotic just to talk to a loved one.

"Oh my God, hi!" I nearly shouted. "How are you?"

She could hear my excitement and giggled. I could also hear my mom in the background, yelling her greeting.

I was smiling and almost in tears when they told me they were on their way to come see me.

"Hey, Ty, you there? You hear me? We're coming to see you," Christina shouted into the phone.

I laughed as the waterworks were on again. I cried more the first week there than I think I ever had in my entire life, except maybe when Grandma Bechel passed away. I was absolutely ecstatic that they were coming to visit. I didn't expect it at all, and Christina didn't say anything the night before.

"How long before you guys get here? Like, hurry up!"

"We should be there in about twenty minutes."

Twenty minutes was an even better surprise. I couldn't believe I was going to get to see them. I wasn't going to get to see my daughters, but Christina and Mom were good enough for the time being.

I couldn't contain my excitement; I was smiling from ear to ear. I was feeling better than I had in years, and I was now experiencing a sense of joy that was so strong that I was reminded of what it was like to be genuinely excited about other people.

I had spent almost an entire decade worrying about my wants, needs, and desires that I completely shut out that little voice in my head that said it is okay to be excited. I was pacing the floors waiting for their arrival; it felt like a child's Christmas morning. My heart was excessively beating, and I couldn't wait to hug them both.

I ran down the hallway to use the bathroom, and one of the staff members said not to run.

"Okay," I stated with a smile as I started speed walking. I didn't want to miss their arrival, because I wanted to greet them even before they stepped out of the car.

I hurried (didn't even wash my hands) ...ran back down the hall...again, I was told "no running"... "sped walked" the rest of the way.

Nothing could have interfered with my joy that day.

Light on my feet from sudden elation, I felt like Spider-Man, or a ninja, jumping down the steps. I could have possibly been so happy that I was having a moment of euphoria. I shoved the back glass door open by the smoking area, and the sunlight hit my face. The sky was blue, and the sun was bright. I could feel the warmth of the big ball of gas warming instantly. I felt so great that I had a quick thought of being in a musical. *The Sound of Music* popped up in my mind when Julie Andrews was dancing and singing in the field. I only like a few musicals (*West Side Story, The Wizard of Oz, Across the Universe, Mary Poppins* [dang it, Julie Andrews], *The Rocky Horror Picture Show, and Repo: The Genetic Opera).*

I ran around the back corner of the building, and I saw Mom and Christina pulling in the graveled parking area. They both smiled and waved. It took them too long to park as I stared at them. They were trapped in this metal box with glass windows, and I wanted to help them escape. Inside my head, my conscious was jumping up and down and clapping. So many thoughts and emotions rushed over me as I impatiently waited for them to get out of the vehicle.

My mom stepped out of the car, and I grabbed her and gave her a big bear hug. I think I almost broke her in half. I ran to Christina and wrapped my arms around her. I held her for a few seconds even though it felt like an hour. Her hair smelled like flowers. I released my death grip of a hug and kissed her.

"Get a room," I heard my mom say.

It was so amazing to see them. It was almost as if I hadn't seen them in years.

Retrospectively, I actually had not seen them in years with all of the drug and alcohol consumption. I believe I was experiencing a raw and organic connection with them for the first time in forever.

I showed them around the building. They made a few comments about it being a bit run down and in bad shape. I had to remind them that inside is where the miracles happen. As we toured the gym, they both said that it didn't look much better inside than it did outside.

I am not exactly sure why I responded the way that I did, but I replied to their criticism.

"It's not about how it looks or what we don't have here, it is about what I do have and that I am in a safe place. I'm not royalty, and this place is perfect. I'll make best with what I have, and I have you two, so that is pretty good."

They both looked at each other, then at me, and smiled.

In just a short time, I had come to realize I was not owed anything, and most of my dissatisfactions in life were the way I viewed the world...and myself. I remember looking around after I told them that the sober living home was perfect and being in awe that I was alive. In that exact moment in time, I was content with myself and who was around me.

Mom and Christina couldn't stay long. They wanted to go into town and eat, but I couldn't because it had to be approved by the director, who was off that day. I was able to ride with them to the convenience store up the street, where Mom bought me a few packs of cigarettes and a couple of energy drinks. I pumped gas for Christina, and that felt right to do.

I know it was only pumping gas, but I was able to do it clean and sober.

They drove me back to the building, and it hit me that we would have to say goodbye. Christina said she was going to come back soon and would bring our daughters. I hugged my mom and thanked her for coming, then I hugged Christina and gave her a kiss goodbye.

I watched them drive away, but I was okay with it. I was right where I needed to be, and I knew I had a lot of more work that needed to be done.

I ran to my room, where I laid on the bed and smiled. It was a beautiful day. I was clean and sober, had food to eat, shelter over my head, and my family had driven over an hour to see me. I could only imagine what else I was going to experience.

Chapter 5
What Matters Most

The next few weeks at my new home were spent making friends and realizing that the energy I put out into the world is the same energy that I attract.

I no longer wanted to be negative; negativity seems easy to find, hard to shake, and like an unwanted traveling partner that you know you have to get away from or risk going mad. Escaping madness isn't possible if we just run and hide.

And that is just what the drugs did—offered a temporary place of sanctuary from the madness. The protection didn't last long and was never real to begin with; rather, it was fabricated safety and falsified enlightenment. I realized that the madness follows you because it has burrowed its way into your mind. Wherever I went, the madness and negativity ensued.

There are many ways that we can deconstruct the insanity that lives comfortably within our being— therapy, meditation, praying, creating (fiction, sculptures, paintings), or taking a hard and honest look at ourselves.

I wasn't exactly sure what form my deconstruction process would take, but I knew that it had to be done. It is very easy for us to continue to run from something that causes suffering and pain, but our legs usually give out, and we eventually become consumed by the monsters right on our tails.

I was doing really well in the house, so Roger, the director, wanted me to be the chore monitor. He sat me down in his office and explained the responsibilities. I was terrified at first, and I think he could tell.

One of the tasks was making sure the rest of the residents were doing their chores properly. When I heard him tell me this, I couldn't fathom at the moment that I would have to enforce the house rules. The word "rules" kept repeating itself in my mind like I was in an echo chamber. I didn't want to be "that guy."

Roger carried on about how it would help strengthen my recovery, and that began to persuade me to accept the position.

Another employee named Mark, who lived in an upstairs bedroom and watched over the house, joined us for the meeting. He was tall and lanky, and you could usually find him carrying around his coffee-filled thermos. He served as kind of the resident "drill instructor," which was good for many of us.

"You can't always take the easier, softer way out all your life," he would say anytime he caught one of us slacking on our responsibilities.

Mark sat down next to me and asked me to take the job.

"Come on, Ty," he pleaded (I think he didn't want to have to do it anymore).

I looked at him and smiled. I wanted to say yes, but I was worried about the residents turning into rabid animals and calling me a brown-noser or a kiss-ass. At least, that was what I would have called someone that was trying to tell me what to do when they weren't any less of a mess than I was.

"Ty, you are always doing your chores and helping out when you don't need to. You will do great," Mark said, doing his best to encourage me.

Roger stared, waiting for an answer. I did believe that our chores should be done right, and I think they knew that. My Grandma Bechel always made sure I did my chores correctly and not half-assed. If I did the dishes and she saw one dish was dirty, she would make me rewash all of the dishes (I can tell you that only happened one time). I guess the impression took root.

As Roger continued to stare at me with that smile, it started to feel like minutes ticking and turning into hours.

"I tell you what, Ty. Sleep on it and let us know tomorrow."

I felt relief. I'd have time to think it over.

I went about my business for the day, but when bedtime came, I still wasn't sure what I was going to do, so I prayed about it and went to bed.

When I woke up, I found myself calm with the idea, so I decided to give it a spin.

After my morning routine, I met Mark, Sally, and Roger in the office, and when I smiled at him, Roger knew what my decision had been, and he assigned Mark to tell me what to do.

Mark grabbed a clipboard and showed me all of the chores that needed to be done. Our chores rotated every week or two, so I was familiar with all of the responsibilities, which involved cleaning the gym, bathrooms, television room and office. He reminded me that since I was going to be the chore monitor, I would not be doing any of these tasks myself. The leadership role was my chore, going from spot to spot and making sure things were up to snuff (and, believe me, it was a *chore.)*

That first week, I was very timid and passive toward the residents. I didn't want to create waves or make anyone upset, but thankfully Mark became a mentor and explained that chores must be done correctly and when expected. His words reminded me of Grandma Bechel.

A lot of small changes had taken place since I arrived at the recovery home. I was feeling healthier and happier. One of my new friends, Jack, became a support to help me discover who I was, who I thought I was, and what I would possibly become if I continued taking necessary steps.

I was feeling great, and then Jimmy, the hanger hero from my first day, was asked to leave the facility. I had grown accustomed to him and his presence, but from my understanding, he had other issues that required a higher level of care, and his continued presence at the home was putting himself, and others, at risk.

Jimmy was the first of many that I would see leave over the course of the next few months.

Christina was bringing our daughters for their first visit. I don't think I slept at all the night before they came, just from sheer excitement. I laid in bed, waiting to get up and eat breakfast.

7:30. I still have more than three hours to go.

I gobbled breakfast like it would somehow speed things up. I was full of energy and couldn't stop pacing. I kept looking out the window, envisioning our car pulling into the parking area and my girls climbing out.

I had to contain my energy before I ended up bursting into a million pieces, so I went to the gym to shoot some hoops. I dribbled the ball...left hand, right hand. The impact of the ball against my hand, followed by the thud when it hit the floor was calming. It took me back to the days before the addiction.

I used to take my car and go to basketball courts and play for hours. I would open up the trunk of my car and put on "hooping" music (stuff like Tupac's *Still Ballin'*). Most of us that showed to the courts picked teams and would play, argue, and play some more.

It felt good remembering that time in my life. After the moment of reflection, I shot the ball...and promptly air-balled it. Laughing, I looked over my shoulder to make sure nobody saw me.

I guess I needed some practice.

11 o'clock finally rolled around...but no Christina. My heart beat loudly - so loud, in fact, I thought it was going to escape my chest. I was giddy and felt like time was moving extra slow. I looked at the clock. Ten after.

Dang it. Where are they?

I looked again. Fourteen after. I kept telling myself to calm down; they would be there shortly.

At twenty minutes after eleven, the car pulled into the lot. I tried to contain my excitement—to be *cool*—but it didn't work very well. Christina opened the back door, and Dorie Mae stepped out. She went to the other side and took Allie Lynn out of her car seat. I ran to the red door and climbed the few steps leading to the car, and I knelt down and hugged my daughters.

The sense of relief, love, sadness, guilt, and sheer joy flooded me. Uncontrollable tears fell from my face.

"Daddy!"

Dorie Mae had just said the best word I'd heard all week. I didn't want to let them go. I kissed them on their cheeks, hugged them again, and kissed their cheeks again. I stood up and kissed Christina, who was crying.

So were Dorie and me.

Allie? Well, she was smiling and laughing.

As we loaded up and the car zoomed down the road, the four-hour day pass I had earned, reuniting me with my family, had me feeling on top of the world.

Chapter 6
The Number One Ingredient

One thing I was learning is that I did not have much control or power over many things, people included. I started working with Jack more frequently; he was teaching me how to live life clean and sober. He helped me realize just how powerless over drugs and alcohol I had become and how I'd allowed the obsession and use of drugs (alcohol included) to dictate my life. I had been utterly powerless.

My primary functions went haywire because my brain was now altered. It made sense that I was out of control when I was putting poison in my body and forcing my brain to choose living life to the fullest or drugs and alcohol.

Not only was I powerless, but Jack also taught me that there is a power that cares about me and wants to see me do well. This authority was a God I could understand. He explained to me that there are many different interpretations of God throughout the world and history. He gave me a big book that I would come to love and use as a way to better understand addiction and my malady.

On the first page, he wrote: G.O.D. – Good Orderly Direction.

I have had many doubts about God over the years. I studied religion and saw how these religions say they want peace but yet hurt one another in the name of different beliefs. In active addiction, this was always one of my personal quarrels - a power that is so paramount wouldn't allow such horrific things to happen in a world it supposedly created.

Throughout my journey in life, I was once an atheist, agnostic, nihilistic, a believer, a nonbeliever, and most importantly, a jerk. Jack helped me realize that human beings can be very mean, but they can also be very kind and beautiful. He led me to believe that there indeed is a power in the universe that loved me and wants me to live a happy life. His kind words made sense to me to help unravel years of confusion and analyzation of such a big topic. He helped me see that I, too, had made some horrible mistakes. He helped me know that I was living a life of contradictions and that if I was angry about what others were doing, then why wasn't I looking inward at those things I did to hurt other people?

After our week-long discussion, a light bulb flickered. It then grew brighter and brighter. Years of anger and argumentative tendencies seemed less important. A sense of peace was present in my life that I only felt when I was with Grandma Bechel. I realized I felt safe, and everything was going to be okay. The feeling that you don't have to fight anyone or anything any longer is almost indescribable. I wanted to discover even more about myself.

Through self-discovery can sometimes come unwarranted moments of horror. Like ziti.

Let me explain. One evening, while I was cooking dinner for the house, I chose to cook baked ziti. I had all of the ingredients and cooking utensils out on the counter. I was excited to cook this dish because pasta is a guilty pleasure of mine and Grandma Bechel taught me that the number one ingredient for any dish or dessert is love. I wanted to make the baked ziti tasty so that the residents would like it.

I grabbed the 32-quart stainless steel pot and filled it with water and a few splashes of olive oil so that the ziti wouldn't stick. I sat it on the stove and turned on the burner. *Click...click...click.* The pilot light must have burned out. I grabbed the lighter from the drawer and turned on the burner again, flicking the lighter. The burner raced with flames.

I went back to the counter and started separating the garlic bread pieces apart and placing them on the large, foil-wrapped cookie sheet. The garlic bread was neatly placed on the cookie sheets, so I started on the salad. I removed the heads of romaine lettuce out of their packaging so I could start cutting it up and prep the dinner salad that included shredded carrots, sliced red cabbage, golden pepperoncini, and some tiny pepperonis.

I was listening to the radio, had a "pep-in-my-step," and was smiling ear to ear. I could hear the light rumble of the water beginning to boil. I went to check the flame. I tilted my head so I could see underneath the pot and lower the flame just right. When I did, I smelled something all too familiar. I didn't want to smell that smell. That smell. I could hear the lyrics from Lynyrd Skynyrd's song "That Smell" running loudly in my head. I started sweating, and my heart started beating more quickly. Thoughts of using rushed toward my mind like a speeding train. My mouth began salivating.

"NO!"

I ran to the kitchen door and slammed it shut. I couldn't let anyone see me like that. The burning smell of the pot caught me off guard and was almost identical to the stench of a flame warming the bottom of a spoon or cut up soda can; I started crying.

"Not today, not fucking today. You don't own me anymore, YOU FUCKING HEAR ME?!"

I was pacing the floor like a madman.

"You're just a stainless-steel pot. You're just a smell, that's all."

I ran to the pantry and shut the door behind me. The fear of a hijacked mind and body of a destructive and familiar pastime of mine was real. I fell to the ground, placing my back against the stand-up freezer. I took a few deep breaths and started praying.

"I need your help. I do not want to be thinking of this drug. It did nothing for me. Please help. Please let everyone like dinner. They deserve a healthy and tasty dinner. Please take this feeling away. Just let me cook their dinner in peace."

I slowly opened my eyes. A calm rushed over me. I took another deep breath and walked into the kitchen. A random song was lightly playing in the background that definitely was NOT "That Smell," and the water in the pot was at a rolling boil. I could hear the background noises, but they were faint, almost muffled. I had the feeling that everything was going to be okay.

I was going to be okay.

And this was going to be the best damn dinner I'd cooked in a long time.

Chapter 7
Menu Tantrums and My "They're All Mine" Moment

It took some time for me to stir up the courage to talk to Jack about what had happened in the kitchen.

When I did, he reminded me that our brains relate scents, places, and even people with memories that can trigger cravings. He reinforced that when we become aware of the power that people, places, and things have over us in the early stages of recovery, we can then begin to make the necessary adjustments needed.

It was a reminder that this was an ongoing journey, and he explained things in a way that I could understand and use on a daily basis.

Nothing he could say would be able to prepare me for the new resident, though.

It was always exciting when a new one came in. The staff would usually tell us whether the newcomer was male or female ahead of time, but that was about it...so it left a lot to the imagination.

I was told that the new resident would be male and that he was going to be in my pod—in Jimmy's old room.

When someone new would move in as a roommate at the sober living home, we always hoped the guy wasn't going to be a dick. We'd hope he was going to do his fair share of cleaning and wouldn't be utterly primitive in laying claim to his newly acquired *land.*

We hoped, but we always knew there was a chance.

The new resident was starting orientation in the office, while a few of us rubberneckers tried to peek through the vertical rectangular window to get a read on him. His back was turned to us, though so we would have to wait until he was done with his paperwork.

We were still lingering in the hallway when the office door opened, and Sally and the new guy came walking toward us. I instantly looked at this man and thought of half a dozen ways to make fun of him. He looked like someone that could take it and dish it right back. His oddly and perfectly round head was razor shaved. He was tall and walked with a slight waddle. He wore glasses and looked nervous as hell.

Sally approached us first.

"Hey, guys! This is our new resident, Josh."

"Hello, Josh," we all clamored.

He smiled and shook our hands one by one.

Sandy didn't hesitate to ask Josh what his drug of choice was. He calmly answered that it was alcohol. We all stood there and chatted for a few minutes, and I decided that I liked Josh already. I could tell he was a smart-ass. I was asked by Sally to help him take his belongings to his room, while she prepared his bedding. We went to the office and grabbed his bags. I carried one, and he carried the other. We went up the two flights of stairs.

And then it started before we had even made it to the top.

"Wait, I gotta walk up and down these every day? And what's with these plants? They look like shit."

There were a variety of sickly looking plants at the top of the first flight of stairs by the big window. None of us were great at pruning and maintaining their health. The leaves were either brown and dead or severely wilted. We couldn't hear their screams for attention and water.

"Hey, I'm not too great at that type of thing, yet. I don't think they will care if you take care of them," I replied.

Josh had a very distinctive high-pitched, fast, and childlike laugh.

"Nah, I just like bitching. Fuck those plants."

I couldn't help but laugh. "Alright, then. Let's get you to your suite, sir."

Josh and I opened the door to the pod, and it lightly creaked. The hardwood floor beneath our feet screamed with old age. I opened the door to his room and invited him in, setting the bag I was holding on the sheet less mattress. He stepped through the door and entered the narrow and rectangular bedroom.

"What the hell kind of room is this? Jail cells are nicer than this!" he proclaimed.

I laughed. I knew that this room was better than a jail cell.

"Well, yeah it's not the greatest, but we eat better than jail," I replied, tapping him on the shoulder, "Get unpacked and Sally will get you your bedding. You might get lucky and get the dinosaur comforter."

He stared at me with confusion. "What the fuck? Dinosaurs?"

I left the room and pod, smiling as I heard Josh mumble obscenities under his breath.

A few weeks after Josh moved in, Roger asked if I wanted to become the kitchen manager. The responsibilities would include planning the house menu weekly, going to the grocery store every Wednesday, and helping any resident that may not be too familiar with cooking. This was a big job to undertake, but I liked it better than being the chore monitor. I accepted the responsibility, and they actually let Josh become the chore monitor.

My newfound facility career was a tedious task. Trying to plan a menu that most of the residents could be satisfied with was a challenge. It never failed; every week when I planned the meals, some resident would complain about one of the options. I witnessed just how negative and unhappy human beings can be, myself included; my first month or so at the house, I'd complained about the meals too.

One afternoon after I printed the menu for everyone so they could select the meals they wanted to cook, a negative cloud must have been present. Nearly everyone opened their mouth and unleashed their invisible vomit. Complaint after complaint filled the room with toxicity and aggression. I was grateful to be alive and offered the opportunity to assist in our house responsibilities, so I couldn't understand why the rest of the house couldn't see that their position wasn't as bad as before their arrival.

I stalked down the hall in anger, flipping the switch and ringing that annoying bell. Most of the residents came into the hall, asking what was going on. I was calling a house meeting.

We all piled into the television room where we would have our morning and recovery meetings. Chatter filled the room. The other residents were uncertain and confused. A few were worried that someone was in trouble.

I sat at the head of the four tables that were placed to form a rectangle table (not nearly as noble as King Arthur's Round Table). Many profound and revealing conversations had happened at our rectangle table before me (and would repeat after me). Tears and fears had been shared at the very table where we were now sitting.

Everyone was waiting for me, while I was saying a quick prayer in my mind. I needed to find the right words; I didn't want to come across as trying to be better than everyone. I took a deep breath, grabbed the newly printed weekly menu off of the table, held it in the air and began speaking.

"I have heard quite a few people complain about the menu to the point of aggressive rhetoric. I do my best to allow everyone to give a meal that they would like to see on the menu. I plan it the best that I can. We have to remember that we have shelter, food, and an opportunity to change our lives for the better."

It felt like I was giving a monologue in some dramatic movie.

My frustration that others couldn't be happy with my efforts came front and center, which, if I am honest, was the fear that I was doing something wrong. I slammed the printed menu down on the table as I scowled.

"If you guys don't like the menu then, guess what, you don't have to eat it!"

I pointed to one of the residents.

"You! Would you like to plan the menu and go shopping at the grocery store for damn near two hours and spend another hour putting the groceries away?"

The resident's eye bugged out of their head, and they quickly shook their head no.

Everyone sitting at that table was quiet. I reinforced that it was not easy trying to balance the menu for everyone's satisfaction. I apologized for shouting, though I was still upset. I grabbed the menu and quietly walked out. Before I stepped out of the room, I left everyone with one more thought.

"Y'all need to count your damn blessings and maybe not act like you're owed something."

After the menu incident, everyone started helping a little bit more frequently. A few residents showed up and helped put away the groceries when Mark and I returned from the store. I reflected on the encounter for some time; I knew I could have handled it a bit better. Most of us in that house wanted some type of happiness or comfort. Hell, most of us used drugs and alcohol that much just trying to create our own happiness. Reality sucked for me once, but I was offered a dose of how lost we can get.

I spoke with Jack on a few occasions about my mild blowup. Each time he calmly explained that it was part of recovery. That was how we learn to navigate the world around us. I felt horrible for shouting, but Jack reassured me that it could have gone worse.

Going home for a "day" actually meant leaving on Friday at nine in the morning and returning by ten on Saturday night. I had been at the house for a while and going home was much needed, and Roger gave me the opportunity. Christina took a day off of work and picked me up on Friday morning. She pulled into the parking area, and I bolted toward the door. I threw my duffle bag in the trunk and opened the door to the backseat, giving Allie and Dorie each a big kiss. I sat in the passenger seat, tightened my seat belt, and kissed Christina.

It felt amazing as we coasted down the highway. I looked at the girls through the mirror on the sun visor, and then I looked at Christina. For one whole day, they were all mine while I was clean and sober.

I don't think I quit smiling the entire time that I was home.

Chapter 8
Going Home

"It's so hard...to say goodbye...to yesterday."

I could relate to this Boyz II Men song because, in a way, I was saying goodbye to a former self that I would only visit when I was busy removing the remaining shards of my destruction from active addiction.

My days were coming to a close at the recovery home. I was still managing the kitchen and food pantry with love and tolerance, getting frustrated from time to time. I was still working with Jack as he was teaching me how to love myself, get closer to a God I could understand, and how to forgive both myself and others. He had me write down everyone that I had hurt in the past, and also write down who had harmed me in any way in the past.

I grabbed my pencil and notepad and began writing. Hmmm...the people I had hurt. I listed Christina, my mom, my brother, my grandmother, my friends, past co-workers, past women, my children, and much more. Within the confinements of this list was also a description of what I had done to them or what had been done to me. For the first time in my life, I took a look at myself – I had always avoided who I was – and now I was able to connect the dots of human irrationality, fear, power struggles (powerlessness), thoughts of being lonely, low self-esteem, and so much more. I was able to bring to life the labyrinth of my life that has been created (partly my fault...and somewhat not). I always believed in the quote by Gandhi, "Be the change you wish to see in the world," but I'd never fully understood it until I was able to begin an honest reflection and examination of myself.

After writing my past transgressions down, like the time I didn't visit Christina the entire time she was pregnant with our oldest daughter, Dorie, and the time I stole my mother's last $50 out of her purse, it was time for me to sit down and share with Jack all that I had written.

As I waited, some of my roommates asked if I was nervous about discussing my past with someone. I wasn't...yet.

The anxiety didn't come until I heard the crunch of tires in the graveled parking area. I gulped nervously. I am not exactly sure why I was getting anxious and nervous all of a sudden. Could it be that I was getting ready to tell another human being everything I'd ever done to others? The fabrication of lies, telling the truth by omission, and creating a reality that is full of fallacious details to make myself look better was over, at least with this one individual.

I hopped up from the flower-patterned couch and ran to the window. I watched Jack get out of his car, adjust his stocking cap to protect his ears from the winter chill, and walk toward the back door of the building. My roommates laughed and poked fun at me, but Josh, my pod mate, encouraged me instead.

I met Jack at the top of the stairs by the office. I believe he could feel the newly acquired tension.

"It's going to be okay, Ty. Promise."

I smiled, notebook in hand, and we walked to the upstairs television area that we called The Great Room. We turned on the lights, shut the double doors for privacy, and sat down—me on one couch and him on another.

He opened up with everything we had worked on together up until that point.

"This part of learning how to live life on life's terms can be tricky," he said with a smile, "but after it's done sincerely, you will fill a weight lift that has been an anchor. Remember, we talked about how out-of-control and powerless we were and are?"

I started to calm down. "Yeah, I remember. We are powerless over drugs, alcohol, even people."

He opened this big book he had brought with him and read an insert. We started talking about the beginning process of believing in a power greater than myself – God, a group of people, even nature. He took me back to three weeks prior when we met and discussed turning our will and our life over to that power that loves us. We discussed faith and what that means. He reinforced that everything we had done so far had been steps, leading up to this exact moment.

I found myself comfortable and relaxed. I felt a presence of safety and friendship.

"Whenever you are ready," he said, to nudge me along.

I looked down at my notebook and opened it up. I stared blankly at the scribbles of pain, guilt, laughter, sadness, despair, fear, and love that I had misused. I looked up from the notebook with tears in my eyes as Jack grinned slightly in a way that told me he knew exactly where I was.

I started with all of the horrible and malicious atrocities I'd committed against Christina and my daughters. Jack would sometimes interject when I would start crying. It was difficult admitting that I gave money to her once, slept with her, and then stole the money back the next morning, sneaking out the door to buy drugs. There were so many confessions of treachery, selfishness, and misdeeds spun into convoluted webs.

It became easier to tell him my past when he shared his experiences, reinforcing that I wasn't alone. Not once did he ever ask, "How dare you treat people that way?" There was also no "you're disgusting" or "you are a piece of trash that deserves to be locked away forever and burn in hell."

The things Jack didn't say are actual comments I've read from social media that pertained to a news article about someone struggling with addiction.

Human beings can be very mean.

I talked with Jack about the women I used for sex, and how I always felt terrible afterward. I discussed yelling at Dorie for no reason while going through withdrawals. I confessed the time I stole money from my grandfather, who had done nothing but love me since I was a child. Jack reinforced how we focus on cleaning our side of the street again.

Before I knew it, almost four hours had gone by. We made it to the last entry of my "personal inventory." It was over. My face stained with salt trails from the many tears that escaped. My shirt on my left and right shoulders were damp from the constant wiping of those tears.

Jack and I stood up from our seats. I sat my notebook down to extend my hand for a very thankful handshake, but I decided, at the last moment, to give Jack a hug. I thanked him over and over as I walked him to the back door.

I made my way to my bedroom. I opened up the pod door as it lightly creaked. The eight or nine steps that it took to get to my pod creaked, waking Josh.

"Hey, asshole, you woke me up," he said, followed by his fast and childlike laugh, "How'd it go with Jack?"

I opened my bedroom door. I pulled back the comforter, changed my clothes, kicked off my shoes, and hopped into bed.

"Hey, dickface...I said, how'd it go with Jack?"

I turned off the light and finally replied to Josh's question.

"It went better than I had imagined it would. Love you, bro."

I heard him rambling on about something, but as I descended into a peaceful sleep, his words became distant and garbled.

I woke the next morning with an instant smile. I slept like I'd never slept before. I felt different.

I felt...*alive*.

I'd kept my past locked away in a dungeon...concealed 50 feet deep in my limbic system, but it couldn't control me anymore. Everything that I was regretful and shameful for became real, not only to another person but to me, as well. I stopped running *from* something and began running *toward* something.

For the next few weeks after telling Jack everything, we worked on my character defects and shortcomings. It was effortless to connect the dots regarding why I had done a lot of the things I did and how I responded to situations.

I started loving myself. The mirrors I avoided at all costs were no longer my enemy, but a friend I could trust to encourage me to enjoy myself and remind me just how far I had come. I was developing active and fulfilling friendships with the ability to care more about what others had to say. I didn't feel like I had to hide any longer.

One of the last things Jack and I worked on was making a list of people I had hurt and who I was willing to make apologies and amends to. Most of the people included on the list were back home in Madison County, Illinois. I didn't want to call people to make amends, I wanted to be directly in front of them if at all possible.

My last day at the recovery home was quickly approaching...March 21. Every year, the house has a St. Patrick's Day celebration. They cook corned beef and cabbage, served with a side of potatoes (and dessert if you something sweet). Since I was in charge of the kitchen, I was tasked with planning and organizing the food and dining room setup. A few of us spent the night of March 20 boiling the corned beef and all of the additional preparations.

It was almost midnight by the time we closed down the kitchen.

I knew I had to get up at 5 a.m. to start preparing the rest of the food. My feet were dragging as I made my way to the bedroom. I was tired, but I couldn't help but think of everything that I had discovered about myself and life in general over the course of nearly seven months. I was getting ready to leave the next day, and I was nervous, excited, terrified, happy, and cautious. I never wanted to use or drink again. I even thought about finally quitting my cigarette habit. I was chewing nicotine gum and confident I could succeed.

I laid in bed...happy, content, joyous, and free. I had my whole life ahead of me. A new humble beginning was approaching. I prayed and thanked the God I understand for helping me this far. I talked with God as my eyes closed. I drifted away.

The following morning, I rushed downstairs to take a shower. Once I was done, I had to go back to my room and pack my bags. The last few things I shoved in my duffle bag were my dirty clothes and pajamas. I am not entirely sure why I focused so much of my attention to that exact moment, but I did. I took a deep breath and had so many thoughts running through my head. I chuckled as

I placed all of the bags in front of the armoire. I had to get back downstairs and start prepping.

After about an hour or so in the kitchen, Josh joined me to help. We had to cut well over 30 pounds of potatoes, 25 heads of cabbage, and slice the boiled corned beef from the previous night to bake.

The rest of the residents started showing up to help. They were straightening tables, plating desserts, and anything else that needed to be done for the event. Including guests, we expected over a hundred people would be attending that day. One of those people would be Christina, and I was looking forward to seeing her and going home to my daughters.

I sat down in the gym where all of the tables and chairs sat empty. It was quiet. I looked around and saw all the work we did together to get everything in order for this yearly event. I knew I was leaving later that afternoon, and a sense of accomplishment washed over me. Not only were the residents and I able to come together for a common purpose, but we also did it without drugs or aggression.

I got up from the chair and walked around. In a few hours, it was going to be packed with the hungry and supportive guests of the recovery home.

It's incredible to be alive.

The time came for the guests to arrive. I was in the kitchen directing traffic, going back and forth to the serving table to see if there was any need for a refill on food. Things were going smoothly. The gymnasium echoed with careless chatter and some laughter. Nobody was revolting and throwing their plates on the ground in disgust. People were shuffling back for seconds. Residents were going around picking up used plates and tossing them in the trash.

WE did good.

Roger walked up to the podium and began thanking everyone for coming before introducing the guest speakers. He was sharing memories he had of the recovery home since he'd begun working there and brought up a past resident that was still doing well. I listened to the brief story, then leaned toward Christina.

"Psst... hey, let's go," I whispered into her ear.

She looked at me with confusion.

"Don't you want to stay and say something to everyone? Roger said he wanted to thank you and wish you well."

"Yeah, I know he does, but that is okay. I don't need recognition. Let's get outta here. I wanna see the girls."

There were a few residents still in the kitchen cleaning up. I hugged them and told them goodbye. Josh, my pod mate, and new friend asked me to keep in touch.

I held back a few tears and walked out the red door and up the stairs.

As I approached the car, I was reminded of my arrival day while the rocks popped underneath my feet with each step. I couldn't help to think about what a journey it had been. I opened the car door and sat down in the passenger seat.

Christina started the engine, and the humming reaffirmed that we were homebound.

Hold on, Dorie and Allie...and drug court.
Here I come.

Chapter 9
The First Madison County Man to Give Birth

OH, MY GOD, I was home! And it was weird. For years, drugs and alcohol were present nearly every day, or I was spending time in treatment and jail. My daughters were now all mine to cook breakfast for, yell at, play video games with, and so much more. Christina was mine to do with whatever I'd like (wink).

(The wink implies cooking her breakfast. Yeah. We will go with that.)

Joking aside, I was home and had to make many adjustments, both mentally and physically. I reported to drug court outpatient groups Monday morning; the counselor looked like Sergeant Hartman from *Full Metal Jacket*. We got everything situated with paperwork and designated the days I needed to check in. A lot had changed since I left for the recovery home.

Now, in drug court, you had to call a color phone line daily, and if your color was called, you had to undergo a drug screen. We also could no longer hang out with other drug court clients directly – running into each other at 12-step recovery group meetings was the limit of our communication.

Oddly enough, I was excited to see Mr. Blanco, my probation officer. Even though he had been stern with me during active addiction, I respected him. The time spent at the recovery home allowed me to reflect on all of the ways he was trying to help me.

To this day, I still share the story of the time we were on the phone when I was actively using. He'd told me he was "seasoned" and that I needed to quit lying, among other things. In other words, no bullshit.

My first appearance in front of the drug court judge went well. She smiled and told me how proud and excited she was for me. I even got to draw a gift from a blue bucket (I picked Swedish Fish).

I understood right then, and there I liked incentives better than I did sanctions.

It was time to move on with my life. I had to continue attending the outpatient groups. Christina and I paid to get my license reinstated. I continued going to 12-step recovery support meetings daily. We got a gym membership. Everything was going fantastically.

Then something happened. Christina's insecurities came forward with full force. As I was attending a 12-step meeting daily, she began worrying about me using again.

I was getting aggravated and felt as if she didn't want me to succeed. We began arguing. The last time we argued this heavily was when I got out of the long-term treatment program, only to decide to get high again. I wanted to make her happy; I did. But I didn't know exactly what I did wrong or what I could do right.

We decided to go to counseling, which turned out to be rather brutal for her. The counselor kept reiterating that I had to go to 12-step meetings, and, unfortunately, I had to put my recovery first. The counselor even pulled a book from her shelf and sat it in front of Christina; it was the same big book Jack gave me to learn from. I can only imagine what was going on through Christina's mind. She'd lost me to the drugs, and now it seemed to her that she was losing me to recovery.

We left the session, never to return.

I was almost done with drug court when, out of the blue, the upper right part of my back (where your kidneys are) began hurting. I knew this feeling all too well. I hadn't had any kidney stones for almost a year, and my thoughts went into fight or flight mode. The aching and throbbing in my back made me cautious and fearful of a relapse.

I told Christina about the pain. She knew I didn't even like taking over the counter medication such as acetaminophen and ibuprofen, unless absolutely necessary.

I kept telling myself that it just had to run its course. The odd and familiar pain started in the morning and worked its way into the evening. It was uncomfortable to sleep. Relief would come when the stone would stop moving for what I could only imagine as a refueling pit stop so it could get even more powerful.

And it did.

Resting in the fetal position I grunted... "Fuck, fuck, fuck" ...as Christina snored. I did my best not to move too much in the bed, but I couldn't help it. The warm sensation of the stone, however big in millimeters, and the stabbing pain was getting closer and closer. I had never really thought of it the way I did that night, and it made me chuckle...*In a way, this is kind of like contractions. The pain is getting closer in between intervals. I wonder if this is kind of like giving birth. I can name this stone Ramone the Stone.*

My moans ended up waking Christina.

"Shut up. I'm trying to sleep!"

I didn't know what to think of that. I was in pain, so I really didn't care that she was up. I was so angry by the constant attack going on inside my body, I wanted her to enjoy my misery, too.

"Whatever, Christina. This hurts soooooo bad. It's your fault I gotta feel this way," I replied, much like she had when she was giving birth to our daughters. "I'm gonna name him Ramone the Stone."

It was quiet. Then, suddenly, she realized what I was implying.

"You're stupid."

Here I was, awake during the witching hour, alone with my weird and pain-driven thoughts. Pain, like love, will sometimes make you crazy.

Christina started snoring again. I couldn't believe it. Here I was, almost giving birth, and she'd abandoned me. I put my knees together and started swaying them back and forth to get some type of relief. I might have been a little more dramatic than necessary in the hope that I'd wake her up again.

I couldn't help but laugh. Christina kicked me out of bed and told me to go to the couch.

In agony, I turned on the television and laid there thinking, praying this stone would just hurry up. I tried watching infomercials to distract me, but that wasn't even working. The dicer thingy was interesting, and if I had my wallet handy, we would now own something that could slice our vegetables twenty different ways.

I was already in pain, and then I started getting hot. You know how sometimes the blanket gets stuck and you want to move it by kicking your feet then it doesn't want to cooperate? That was me at about 4 a.m. I did the best bicycle air kicks I could, but the blanket defeated me. I didn't have the energy to go on. My predicament worsened. I was hurting more, now sweating, and I really wanted to buy something from the infomercial guy.

"Dammit!"

I was aggravated and wanted this demon child out of my urinary tract. I hated Ramone the Stone more and more as each second passed. I pathetically rolled off of the couch. I walked/limped to get a glass of water. I thought if I drank a lot, the stone would decide it was time to go.

By 7 a.m., the pain was excruciating. I was hurting so badly that I wanted to punch myself in my own throat to distract me from the Battle of Urethra. I went to sit on the toilet. Arms crossed and hunched over, I howled with pain, seriously howled.

"Shut up, sissy," I heard from a distant and faraway land. I could hear her laughing at my misery and the pain that bore me asunder.

"Make it stop," I grumbled.

"Drink water."

I was appalled by this statement.

"What, do you think I'm dumb? I already tried flooding this beast inside me."

I could feel the burning and tingle a few inches above my bladder, and I knew I was almost there.

"Come hold my hand. It's almost time," I pleaded with Christina.

She let out an evil laugh that kind of scared me.

"You're dumb. It's a stone." (Followed by more insidious laughter.)

"OH. MY. GOD! It's here!!" I wailed. The moment of truth when the stone finally passes through the exit. It felt like the head of a Morningstar was scraping the inside of my penis. Someone was taking a steel scratch pad and torturing me.

"Ahhhhhh!" I moaned.

Finally, the deed was done. Ramone the Stone had joined the earthly realm. I breathed a sigh of relief and cradled myself, mumbling, "Thank you, God, thank you."

I happened to look up to my right from being hunched over. Christina was gawking at me.

"What?"

She continued to blankly stare at me, then shook her head and grinned.

"Drama queen."

She turned, in preparation to walk away, and casually tossed over her shoulder, "Oh, by the way, I'm pregnant."

My eyes bulged. My stomach sank. I was still sitting on the toilet, so I quickly grabbed the trash can...and promptly threw up. Some could say it was from the dramatic and terrifying incident from the Battle of Urethra, but fear filled me up in an instant.

I wasn't sure what to think of the shocking news I'd just received. I had not had the time to fully adjust from Ramone the Stone, and here I find out another baby was on the way.

And then, my ass planted on the toilet seat, I realized...

I'd just made it through a harrowing experience...*and hadn't thought about getting drunk or high.*

Looking back, I am pretty confident that the day I returned to Madison County from the recovery home was the day Christina became pregnant.

I prayed and thanked God for helping see me through the situation. Even though I was full of fear about how we would take care of another child, I felt relatively okay with the news. I was going to be a father... again!

Chapter 10
The Great Reconstruction

The Madison County Drug Court program had the graduation event for those of us that had made it through successfully. It was kind of nice to be able to accomplish something after such an extended period of creating paths of destruction. Part of my success was due to Drug Court. It was a tough program, but something a guy like me in the condition I was in needed.

The judge gave us a coin that had an encouraging phrase inscribed on it, a card congratulating us, and the legal document that said our charges had either been dismissed or amended. I had my entire life ahead of me. I watched the people there to support us, like the treatment team from where I did my outpatient groups and a few of my friends and family members.

I sat in the jury box, wondering what was going to happen next. It was my turn to come up to the podium to say a few things about my journey in drug court. At one time, no one thought I would make it. After suicide attempts, many stints in jail, and chronic relapses, I'd proven them wrong. I had more than a year clean and sober, and what felt like an eternity was another memory that I could store away.

I am laughing as I type this...most people that know me understand that I talk a lot. My brain is just busy; I have so much to say and discuss. But as I made it to the podium – tears in my eyes – I only spoke for a few seconds. I thanked everyone, including God, and reminded myself, and those in attendance, that the reconstruction of my life wasn't over.

A few months went by. I was still regularly talking with Jack from the recovery house on the phone about living life on life's terms. He wanted me to start looking for someone to work with that was closer to me. I was okay with that but hesitant. Who would I choose?

I was going to family members and making amends for some of the selfish acts I had committed against them. I made direct amends and explained precisely why I was apologizing. Everyone seemed to accept my formal decision, and I felt great that I could forgive myself for what I had done to them. I didn't necessarily go and find everyone I needed to make amends to, but any chance I was presented to do so, I did.

I was going to many 12-step meetings. Our new baby was due in a few months. It was time I started looking for a job. It had been such a long time since I had last worked—I was pretty nervous; so many critical life-altering things going on at once.

I was nervous about a lot of things; filling out the job application was one of them.

You know what was causing the anxiety - *the question*.

The question terrified me to the point that I'd stop filling out applications when I came to it. Some of you may already know what *the question* is, but if you're scratching your head...

Have you ever been convicted of a crime?

Rejection was still a funky thought that lingered. This particular *question* left me feeling rejected without even being rejected. Jack and I talked about this several times. He always reminded me that God would take care of it, and his words of comfort helped. I started filling out as many applications as I could. It didn't matter where it was – fast food, retail, service.

After escaping the grips of destruction and addiction, I had developed a robust and reliant relationship with a God that I could understand, and that had come and continues every day with a lot of reflection and thinking. I realized that in every job I'd had before, I'd spiraled out of control because of someone I knew.

I wanted to be able to get a job on my own.

I wasn't getting any calls back. Follow-ups always ended up with someone telling me they would be in touch. No one ever was.

Christina's cousin tried to help (so much for doing it on my own). This conversation gave me the opportunity to apologize to him for copping an attitude with him in the past and attending functions at his house under the influence of heroin and other stuff. Like most people, he said not to worry, but I still needed to let him know.

He said he could probably get me hired on as a factory worker where he worked in St. Louis and would check with his boss.

About a week later, he called.

"What's up, buddy?" he asked.

I was hoping he had good news. "Not much. What's going on with you?"

"I think we can get you on at my work as a machine operator. It doesn't pay well, though. I want you to know that."

I was smiling ear-to-ear. The pay didn't matter; it was a job. Someone was going to give me a chance. I thanked him over and over.

The position was a temp-to-hire, so I had to go to an employment temp agency. I would work ninety days and have the opportunity to be hired on the payroll of the actual company if all went well.

I didn't waste any time. I went and filled out the paperwork. I was honest about my background, and I did the employer's drug test without complaint (I passed). I was told to report to the location the following Monday. They gave me the address on a piece of paper, and as I stared at the geographical location, my stomach sank to my feet. Panic overwhelmed me as I flatly stared at the piece of paper.

The location was on Broadway in St. Louis – dead center to where I would travel almost daily to buy my dope.

The staff member asked if I was okay. Of course, I didn't explain to them what was going on in my head. I sheepishly replied that I was okay, grabbed my paperwork, and walked to the car.

I drove home in a daze. I couldn't help but think that I finally had an opportunity to work; irony was playing some sick joke that afternoon. I talked with a new gentleman I was working with that was helping me learn to "live life on life's terms." We came to the conclusion that I had faith in God and this was just a job on a street. I didn't have to let the location represent any of the thoughts that I was having.

After some needed discussion, and much more needed prayer, Monday came for me to start. I had my lunch packed and was ready to go. I showed up to the business and took a deep breath before walking in.

It was strange. I was working a paid job for the first time in a very long time. My new co-worker quickly showed me around and walked me to the machine I would be manning.

I was excited for the first hour.

This mundane task was *boring*. I had to stand in one place, checking for imperfections in the part that was being molded in this gigantic machine. No music. No one to talk to. I couldn't walk around. *How do people do this?* I thought. I looked around at the other machine operators. They all looked okay doing it. Internally, a circus wanted to come out and play. If anyone was going to torture me, making me sit still and be quiet was probably the best way. I couldn't even sit still in the waiting room at a doctor's office.

Ugh… I hated the job, and I hadn't even been there a full eight hours. Looking at these parts hour after hour after hour and shoving them in boxes was excruciating. After my first shift ended, it was 11 at night. I walked out the back door toward my vehicle, feeling the brisk night air on my face. I opened the car door and surveyed my surroundings. We parked inside an enclosed fence that was locked. Shit, I was only three minutes away from Salisbury, ten minutes away from Grand…less than fifteen minutes from any dope that I wanted.

"Stop it!"

I got in my vehicle and put the key in the ignition, taking a deep breath. I said a quick prayer. "Yo, God, get me home."

I positioned my vehicle to press the button for the fence to open, and I made a right onto Broadway. I drove, hoping every stop light would just be green. Every light was green until I came to the one that allowed me to either turn left to go deeper into the city or turn right to cross the bridge that would take me back to the Illinois side (and safety).

I turned right onto the bridge and shouted in victory, hitting the steering wheel. "Fuck YEAH!"

I knew right then and there that drugs didn't control me any longer.

I didn't stay in this job position very long—only about a month. The standing in one place was painful for me, so I put in my two weeks. The temp agency said that I didn't have to go back. I was kind of upset that I was jobless again, but relieved I didn't have to stand in one place for so long.

After about two weeks of unemployment, the temp agency called. They had another position they thought would be more fitting—an office job, helping with sales and customer service. The agency scheduled an interview with the owners and gave me the address.

After the staff member rattled off the address, I screamed inside my head, *What the HELL!?*

This business was in St. Louis, too...also close to a drug-infested area. I told them I would show up when they wanted me there. I knew I could do it, but the irony was crazy. I ended the call and just laughed.

"Do you have some type of sense of humor?" I asked God.

I went to the interview and met the owner, his wife, and the office manager. The interview went fantastically. I was in my comfort zone. Office supplies, phones ringing, filing cabinets, etc. They said they would let me know about the position and reminded me that they had a few other people to interview.

I didn't even get home before my phone rang. It was the temp agency letting me know that I'd gotten the job. I was to start the following week.

Christina was excited when I told her the news. She was due in about a month, and my new employer was understanding. They said I could take a few days off once Christina had our child (I say "child" because we decided to let the gender be a surprise until the delivery day came).

She was hoping for a boy; I was hoping for a miracle. I just wanted to be a good father.

This new job paid almost three dollars more an hour than the last one, and I would be working from 8 to 4. I got my own desk, computer, email, and login password.

I showed up fifteen minutes early that first day, ready to learn and work. The office manager started showing me around the building, taking me to the recycling area, the loading dock, and the drum washing building. She said she would need to drive me to the second location, where they would wash the IBCs (Intermediate Bulk Containers...large, square plastic containers housed in a steel or aluminum cage that are used to store liquids). The company dealt a lot with recycling, washing and reselling 55-gallon polyurethane drums and IBCs.

After about two weeks, Christina's doctor told us that if her water had not broken by March 28, he would like to induce labor. It didn't break, and we were off to the hospital. My new child was going to be here soon, and everyone was excited, even our daughters.

I was about nineteen months or so into recovery, scared shitless, but ready to take on fatherhood one more time. We made our way to the hospital, got settled in, and the doctor showed up. Soon our son or daughter was going to be here, and this time I was stone cold sober.

Chapter 11
The Great Reconstruction, Part Two

"Doctor, nurse, somebody hurry!"

It had been a few hours since the doctor had induced, and Christina laid flat on her back. Her eyes closed as she gripped a piece of the white sheet in her hand.

"Holy shit, you're shaking." She looked up from the bed and made eye contact with me. She must have cast a magic stare or something because I felt my soul quiver. The baby was coming. The nurse got on the phone to track down the doctor. He was still at his office, seeing patients.

I wasn't sure what that meant. The baby could arrive any minute. The nurse started shouting orders. She ran out of the room and came back with a cart full of doctor stuff. She sat Christina up, pulled out the stirrups, and started prepping for delivery.

"Holy hell! What do we do? What the hell do I do?" I could only stare at how quickly the nurse was moving and how badly Christina was shaking.

Ramone the Stone paled by comparison.

Inside my head, my "mini-me" was running around, preparing for a disaster. I suddenly entered tunnel vision. All the noises around me faded as I watched.

The nurse had to snap her fingers to get my attention. "Ty! You are going to have to hold Christina's leg."

I had an idea what that meant, but I didn't want to believe it.

"Wait...what? Why?" I squeaked.

The nurse looked at me very sternly. "We are going to have to deliver this baby."

I laughed; one of those laughs where you are scared, but you laugh to try to let others know that you've got it together...when you really don't.

"OKAY!" I replied, too loudly.

The nurse unfolded a large cloth to place underneath Christina, then put on long, yellowish latex gloves that went almost up to her shoulder.

"Okay, Christina I have delivered a few babies, and the doctor is on his way."

"Hold on, can't we just tell this baby to wait a little longer? I mean, it's been nine months. What're a few more minutes going to hurt?" I pleaded, like a guy would plead.

The nurse gave me a confused and almost disgusted look.

"It's alright, I've done this before." I guess she was trying to assure me we will be okay.

"Okay, you ready, Christina? On the count of three, we are going to do a big push. One...two..."

My mind was in overdrive. *This kid needs some patience.* Axl Rose started whistling the intro to Guns N' Roses' "Patience" in my head.

Ty, what is wrong with you?

Before the nurse made it to three, the doctor walked in.

"Hallelujah!" I shouted to the gods.

"What do we have going on here? You couldn't wait until I got here?" he joked to Christina, as he put on his gloves, gown, and mask with this plastic piece guarding his face. *What's up with the mask? Is shit about to get serious?* I didn't remember the doctor wearing a mask with her other deliveries.

Then my silly thoughts were over, and Christina was pushing. The head was crowning. When I hear people say birth is beautiful, I have to wonder if they have ever been in the trenches; this ordeal was terrifying and traumatic. You would think that since I write horror and love watching horror movies, I would be okay with it. Well... real life horror terrifies me. And this *beautiful* moment made me wonder if we could employ storks once again.

The baby was coming. It had a little bit of hair. Christina yelled as I moved back to hold her leg.

"Okay, one more final push and we are there. One... two... three... and push!"

The head appeared, followed by the shoulders, arms, legs, and even ten little toes. The doctor quickly grabbed the bulb syringe to suction some of the liquid out of the baby's mouth. It was taking longer for the baby to cry than it did with my daughters, and Christina was starting to worry.

The doctor started getting more intense with his movements, mumbling something I couldn't make out.

Oh, God...

Then...

Wa...wa...waaaaaa!!!

The doctor looked at us and asked if we wanted to know the gender. "It's a boy!"

Christina and I looked at each other, and I felt a couple of tears fall down my face. Overwhelmed with joy that he had finally cried, my chest was heavy and almost convulsed from the emotions conjured up from the moment. I grabbed the scissors to cut the umbilical cord.

The doctor and nurse were fantastic. They both smiled and congratulated us. We had a new son, Bryce Andrew. A new Bechel boy was in the world. The polar ice caps might have melted a bit, and universes collided that day. Bryce Andrew was beautiful. The moments before were quite scary, but now I had a son.

The house was busy for a few weeks with visitors stopping by daily. My mom came over nearly every day. She wasn't doing well financially and was about to go through foreclosure on the first home she'd bought. She was upset, buried in debt, and not sure where she was going to go once the foreclosure was final.

I talked to Christina about my mom moving in with us. We lived in a 1,000-square-foot home, but we could manage to be packed like sardines for a little while. Mom was relieved, and I think excited as well, to have a temporary solution.

To make her feel more welcome, I got her a greeting card with a house and shed key tucked inside. I know what is like to feel uncomfortable in another person's home, and I didn't want her to feel that way at all. Of course, my mom's tear duct dam broke, and she cried reading the card. The day came, and we began our cohabitation experiment.

It is comical how life will always throw *life* at you.

I was enjoying my new job; I was able to meet a lot of great workers. One day, trying to make sure a 55-gallon steel drum order was ready for a loyal customer, I had to go help the dock workers get the drums off of one tractor-trailer and placed at the open dock door to load. We were moving quickly, and I was stepping in the tractor-trailer and pulling the steel drums out one by one.

We only had two or three more to pull off of the trailer when I stepped in to grab one of the final drums, and my leg fell through a one-foot gap between the trailer and the dock. My body was guided by gravity, and my left thigh filled the gap, the added weight of my 230-

pound frame wedging me into place. It instantly hurt very badly; I felt the pain all the way to the bone. I'd also hit my testicles on the dock floor and bruised my right wrist trying to stop the fall.

A few of the dock workers helped get me out. Thoughts of pain pills ran rampant. I kept praying, as the workers were helping me, that I wouldn't start thinking I needed anything to take the *edge* off.

The pain lessened and I went home for the day.

I returned to work the following day, even though my leg still was still in pain, and managed a full day before I went home.

By the weekend, my thigh was red with what looked like an infection, and I was having trouble walking and bending, so I went to the hospital. As they broke the news it was, in fact, an infection, I was upfront with the nurse about being in recovery. I didn't want any narcotics—and they didn't give me any.

I went home with antibiotics and directions to keep my leg up to minimize the swelling, but the swelling and pain just kept getting worse. By Sunday, I couldn't even get out of bed, so there was no way I would be able to work the next day. Instead, when Christina went to work that morning, I trekked back to the hospital.

I decided to try a different local hospital, but I followed the same routine. I told the nurse at registration that I was in recovery and I didn't want any narcotics. My thigh must have been severely compromised. I was taken to the back quickly and had multiple doctors come to see me. The bright red color on my leg had moved all the way up my inner thigh – it was almost to my groin – and down past my kneecap.

I was put on an IV of fluid antibiotics, but after an hour or two, my fever spiked. I started shaking. Christina's mom, Beckie, one of the biggest assets in my life, called Christina at work.

I was becoming incoherent, and the doctors said I was going into shock. A surgeon came in and observed my leg. They determined they would have to operate to take some of the fluid off of my leg and get some of the infection out. There was a risk of blood clots, too.

As soon as they got my fever under control, they prepped me for surgery. I met with the anesthesiologist, and she told me the medication they would give me (a small dose) of was fentanyl. My heart immediately sank, and I became enraged. I told her no. I couldn't have it; I was in recovery.

She attempted to explain it was a small dose. I said no. She said I would need the strong narcotic. I said no. She left aggravated.

The nurses gave me medication to put me to sleep. I said goodbye to Christina, lying flat on my back, looking up at the hospital ceiling and praying that I would not want narcotics. The nurses rolled me through the hallways and, somewhere along the way, I fell asleep.

A few hours later, my eyes fluttered open. I was in a small recovery room and could hear the beeps of the medical equipment going off in the background. I knew where I was and was very curious as to what they found during surgery.

My leg was throbbing and all bandaged up. I wasn't really nauseous; I was famished. Christina made her way to the recovery room, and the surgeon joined us shortly after her arrival. The surgeon was relatively young, black hair slightly parted to the side, and very polite. He explained to us that I had a lot of infection in my leg and a golf ball-sized blood clot that had to be removed. He kept rambling on about how lucky I was that I came in when I did, but my primary focus shifted to food.

His speech ended with the declaration that I would have to stay in the hospital a day or two because my six-inch open incision would have to be unpacked and repacked with sterile gauze every six or eight hours by a wound nurse.

He asked me what my pain was on a scale of 1 to 10. I told him probably a 7 (In reality, it was more like a 10). I knew why he was asking that question. Before finding recovery, I would exaggerate my pain scale at any hospital visit – if I said a 9 it was actually a 3. Today was different. I understood fully the destruction that occurred in my life and the pain I felt in my leg was nothing compared to what I had put myself and my family through. I explained to him I only wanted ibuprofen.

Eventually, I was moved to a private room, which meant I was able to eat. I was excited...until I found out the wound nurse would be in soon to change the dressings in my leg.

I ate the food Christina brought me in about 3.2 seconds. As I finished, the room turned dark...thunder clapped...and then *she* entered the room with her box of torture. She introduced herself and was very kind, so I knew she was up to something. She was from the dark forces, sent to create even more pain than I was in already.

She carefully explained the procedure. "I will be removing the old gauze that is packed in the wound, then I will flush it out with this here liquid. The final steps will be to measure your wound and repack it with fresh and sterile gauze."

I told her I'd take her word for it.

My eyes were fixated on the entire process, and so were Christina's. Christina is gross anyway; she likes to watch surgery and those pimple popping videos.

The nurse cut the large bandage that protected the gauze-packed incision. It was a bloody mess, and you could see the gauze packed tightly into this hole that might as well been a cavern. She told me to brace myself as her black hair and eyes turned to flames. A demonic laugh exited her windpipes, and I prayed this wasn't the apocalypse.

She began pulling the old gauze out. I gripped the blanket with both hands and screamed.

"I hate you! Who are you, lady? STOP!"

She looked at me, and then at Christina. They both started laughing.

"It will be over soon, I promise."

I closed my eyes. The nurse continued to remove the old gauze. "FUCK! I hate you, lady! Well, I'm sorry, you are nice, but this hurts…fuck! Go back to the abyss you escaped from, you treacherous monster!"

They both laughed even harder. The nurse even snorted.

Eventually, her evil game was done, and I apologized for screaming for mercy. She asked me my pain level, and I told her I only needed ibuprofen.

It was quite nerve-wracking being in the hospital. Every nurse at shift change would ask me my pain level and if I needed stronger medication. It got annoying, and I told one in no uncertain terms that I did not want to be asked again.

And then, finally, I was discharged.

I got into the car and started thumbing through the discharge paperwork and any follow-up instructions. I pulled out the prescription paperwork.

I couldn't believe my eyes. I couldn't believe what they'd prescribed me, and my anger and confusion exploded. Why would they prescribe something to me when I explicitly told them that I was in recovery and I wanted no narcotics? I looked at the prescription again in disgust. They sent a recovering alcoholic/addict - who had spent his last two years in active addiction heavily sedated on strong and illicit opiates like heroin and fentanyl - home with something that could take him right back to the streets of St. Louis and the county jail.

I couldn't quit staring at the prescription. Percocet...sixty of them...could have been all mine.

With one refill, if I'd wanted it.

Christina startled me by touching my arm. "You're not going to get that filled, are you?"

I shook my head in disbelief. Not at her, but at the entrance to death they had sent home with me.

"Hell no. I know damn good, and well I cannot take these. Seriously, why would the hospital do that?"

I ripped it up. Every tear of that paper was a statement...a statement of determination to continue seeking recovery. My brow crinkled in aggravation. My chest tightened with dedication. *Not today,* I told myself.

Some of the most significant changes in my life were yet to come, and I believe that that moment gave me the fuel of confidence I needed. Change was getting ready to become one of my best friends.

Chapter 12
The Great Reconstruction...The Final Chapter

Changes in my life were moving quickly.

A few weeks after returning home from the hospital, Christina sat me down and said she needed to talk. She was holding Bryce in her arms as he quietly drank his bottle.

First, she told me we were offered the bigger house we had wanted to get before I got hurt. But something else was bothering her. Her eyes were different than usual; she was worried.

"I have something else I have to tell you, too," she said with a slight quiver in her voice.

I couldn't help but think ten thousand of the worst thoughts. *Is she going to leave me? Did she cheat on me? Does she have something wrong with her medically?*

It was like a semi-automatic gun of thoughts firing in my mind.

My posture straightened, and palms began to sweat. "Well, what is it?"

Her eyes filled with tears. I wasn't sure what was going on. *Maybe she burnt the meatloaf and was just really looking forward to meatloaf,* I thought to myself. I was trying to find comedic relief in an uncomfortable situation.

She finally answered me. "I... I burned the meatloaf," she stuttered.

Ha! Who I am kidding? What she really said was, "Ty, I'm pregnant again."

My jaw dropped. I wasn't sure what to do or say. She was worried and crying, and all I could think was *how are we going to pull this off.* I was instantly nauseous. I got the feeling you get when an elevator goes down too fast. Anxiety in my chest was tightly bound around any logic or reason.

I wasn't sure about anything.

A few weeks went by after Christina broke the big news, and it was time to move into our new home. Bigger, nicer, and more expensive, the brick house was just a few blocks down from where I grew up with my Grandma Bechel.

I was excited to be back in the neighborhood. I couldn't help move anything because my leg was still packed with gauze, so it was fun to sit in a chair and bark orders. Everyone helping to move us just ignored me.

Shortly after moving in, a source from my job in St. Louis told me the owners weren't planning to pay any of my lost wages or cover my medical bills. I wasn't sure what to do.

It soon started to get ugly. I would get emails that were rude, to say the least. I got rumblings that once I returned to work, the owners were planning to do everything they could to make my job difficult. They were behaving as if I had turned in my two weeks' notice.

Again, I wasn't sure what to do.

I prayed about the situation. I talked about it to numerous people; I really loved my job and the people, and I didn't want to leave. I feared heavy retaliation from the owners, so I decided not to return on my first day back.

I was stepping away from the first job I'd found while in recovery that I had actually enjoyed. It was becoming more and more evident that a new house, a new child on the way, and a new way of living without drugs and alcohol were allowing me to handle situations differently than I would have in the past, but I was still scared.

My life felt like something out of a movie. I continued to go to 12-step meetings and found understanding and peace in listening and sharing with others. Reflection became a big part of my morning. I started waking up at four in the morning so that I could walk and spend time talking with God.

On one of those mornings, I was listening to some music. I had a thought about starting an organization that could work with those in early recovery or those seeking recovery from drug and alcohol addiction, while also assisting our community. The doubts instantly surfaced, telling me it would never work.

The next morning, I took my usual walk. As the earbuds pumped Breaking Benjamin into my brain, that thought of creating an organization returned. Like the day before, it was followed by instant doubt. But this time, I started running through questions in my mind.

How would I start the organization? How would I fund it? Who would even want to get involved?

When I got home, I talked about my idea to Christina. Even she was doubtful, so I pushed it to the back of my mind, along with so many other visions and ideas.

The following morning, it was back again. I stopped and looked up at the moon, not yet disappearing into the landscape. It was full and almost amber color. A stray cloud passed over it as I stared and reflected. Sometimes, we get the feeling that everything is going to be okay and the path we are on is where we were intended to be our whole lives. We took a few detours, got lost along the way, but managed to finally stop and ask for directions. I made my way back home.

I unzipped my yellow jacket and sat down at the computer. I wasn't working yet, so I had time to do some research on how to start a not-for-profit. A cup of coffee, a pen and a notepad, and my computer soon became morning visitors after my daily walk. I was brainstorming many different ideas that could alleviate and help mitigate the consequences of addiction on the individual, their family, and the community. I kept in the front of my mind that people have to want to change so that change can start taking place.

I came up with my first slogan. Empower, Educate, Evolve.

It was bizarre. I was taken back to fifth grade, where I was asked what I wanted to do with my life and I replied, "I want to make a difference."

I began looking into state statutes for not-for-profit business entities and website design companies. I was creating different program and service ideas. One program I wanted to create was called *Catch a Ride, not a Case*. The program would have assisted those that needed rides to recovery support meetings, but that would require a car and insurance. The idea would have been just to assist the individuals until they could network and begin getting rides from other people in the meetings they were attending.

When my mom heard about what I was attempting to do, she talked with a woman she knew that was familiar with not-for-profits. I set up my first meeting for a concept about which I was scared shitless, but the compelling feeling to move forward seemed to grow stronger every day. During my morning walks, I would continue to pray and ask if this is where I was supposed to be heading.

I walked into the restaurant in Bethalto for my first of many "official" meetings about the idea.

"Ty, so glad to meet you," the woman said as she shook my hand. "Your mother has told me so much."

I couldn't help but smile, because the feeling of being warmly welcomed was different from the life of active addiction. I sat down and pulled out my notebook jammed with ideas to make Madison County a better and healthier county. We talked for two hours, and she gave me inside tips of what to expect in filing paperwork with state and federal agencies. She explained how a chamber of commerce worked, and why those are so important for networking and finding support for the mission of the not-for-profit.

This woman really had a passion for people who wanted to turn their lives around. She relayed stories of working with people in another state that were getting out of prison and needed help developing job skills and finding gainful employment. I realized this could actually work.

I couldn't believe it. I was embarking on a business plan that had the potential to aid our communities. I was becoming more aware of the sickness that was no longer hiding in dark corners. I prayed time and time again for guidance and strength. I left the breakfast meeting with ideas, drive, and motivation to move forward with what would later become Amare, NFP.

The support she gave at that breakfast morning meeting was beyond crucial, not only to the success of the organization but to my confidence as a human being.

Before my addiction forced me down a deep, dark rabbit hole, I worked in sales and marketing. It was now time to take part in my experience as a "professional" talker and network with people that would advance the mission.

I stood in our garage, scared, trying to summon the courage to make the phone call to a pastor I had never even met. I was given his name and number by someone who said he was very supportive of people getting well and escaping the grips of addiction. Not everyone is welcoming of an honest story of heroin addiction, but I took a shaky breath and dialed his number.

A ring. Two rings. A click.

"Hello, this is Pastor Mark."

I cleared my throat.

"Hi, uhm... I was...uhm...sorry. I was given your name and number from someone that said you might be able to help me."

It was silent. I wasn't sure why he wasn't saying anything.

"Sorry, Ty, I dropped the phone. What is it you are trying to do?"

I explained I was looking for allies and described my vision for the organization.

"I like making allies, tell me more about Amare."

I relaxed. We spent 45 minutes talking, sharing, laughing, and even tearing up a time or two. The conviction of love and of God was in this man's every word. We decided to meet in person at a local coffee shop, and have been friends from that day onward. I was told that in recovery if I keep working at it and remain open-minded and willing daily, that my current relationships will be restored and new relationships that would typically be non-existent would develop.

The love, the grace, the unbelievable power of a heart transformed by an act of providence is beyond words. It is a feeling almost indescribable. It is, in my opinion, something we feel, and we want to share with the world. I was growing. I was evolving. I was beginning to understand *love*.

I wanted to take the pain of all the world and take that experience and turn it into a better life for everyone. I would learn, sadly, that sometimes the human spirit is soaked in hate, but I wouldn't let that deter my mission. I stayed vigilant. I remained persistent. Most importantly, I stayed (and continue to stay) connected to a power greater than myself. Life, as I knew it, was getting ready to become something I could have never fathomed.

I was coming up on two years clean and sober, and I was getting ready to start a state recognized not-for-profit. The fear of rejection from the community and the fear of failing weighed heavy on my thoughts...but prayer and a little bit of action go a long way.

Chapter 13
What Dimension is This?

Let me interject for a moment with a note to my readers.

If you are still reading, thank you.

The time had come. Christina was ready to give birth to our fourth (and this time, for real and for true, without a doubt, *final*) child.

We knew this kid was going to be a boy, so we had all the clothes picked out. The mother-to-be was going to be induced again, but this time they were prepared for the doctor to be more readily available than he was with our first son's birth. I couldn't help but think how close in age the brothers would be...only eleven months apart.

I was scared that I wouldn't be able to be a good father, but I was going to try.

The birth of Brody James went smoothly. I cut the umbilical cord, they cleaned him up, and he was swaddled. They handed our precious child to Christina, and I looked down to see my new son. I couldn't help but laugh.

"Oh. My. God! He looks just like a Bechel!"

Christina, at first irritated, couldn't deny the striking resemblance to the Bechel DNA genetic code, and she chuckled.

"He looks like we cloned you!"

Like my other three children, Brody James was awesome and beautiful.

Family joined us and welcomed us at home. Everyone sat around, passing Brody back and forth so that they could give him love and attention. It was more than I could have ever hoped for; I was more than two years clean and sober, and basking in the moment. My mother, aunts, uncles, Christina, and children filled the living room with laughter, a few tears, and reverence for one another.

The connection we have as human beings that is so tangled in an invisible but powerful energy filled the living room that day. I honestly felt blessed beyond measure.

Later that night, I gave my eleven-month-old son, Bryce, a bath. I remember putting a dab of baby soap in my palm. His eyes were big and bright. He smiled like I said something funny. I grabbed his right foot and started washing it. His little toes curled, I guess from the tickling sensation on the bottom of his foot. I grabbed his left foot. His toes curled again, and he giggled.

"You're pretty dang cool, you know that?' I said, rinsing his hair.

He looked at me and smiled almost as if he understood what I had just said. I couldn't help but think of all the moments I had squandered with drugs, alcohol, anger, and an unwillingness to make the world around me a better place.

I think a lot of us, addict or not, will lose moments because of our ignorance, or at least I did. I am not calling anyone ignorant, but as a people, we tend to forget ourselves in unnecessary desires and beliefs. We become so selfish and self-centered that we hurt people and miss out on the joys and wonders of this human experience we have been given. We tend to put our efforts in something that is synthetic rather than helping one another. We become easily distracted and forget that we can help and care for one another.

We are seeing this today, with the topsy-turvy political climate into which we have been thrust.

But, who I am to preach? I was only able to learn this from the adversity I faced. I was able to experience negative energy on the daily. When I realized most of my problems were of my own making, I was able to open my eyes and heart to the positive energy that is graciously ours if we choose to invite it into our lives.

My children have taught me a lot. They taught me to view time as a privilege, and that nothing seems to be guaranteed in this existence.

My dad lived a few streets down from us. We began talking and slowly began to rebuild a relationship. Even though we had a lot of rough patches growing up – some his fault and some mine – I love him, and God brought a father and son back together. I was able to hear and accept an apology from the years of uncertainty and angst. My father is a great man...with the same demons many of us face.

He would plop onto his riding lawnmower to my house and cut our grass. We began having fun together and giving each other a hard time...just like Bechels tend to do. He started helping me with the garden I started, giving me tips he had learned from years of gardening himself.

My relationships were being restored, and I wouldn't have had this opportunity had I not decided to get clean and sober and turn my will over to the care of a God that I understood.

One of the people that helped me on this road of discovery was my younger brother, Brandon. In my darker hours, I stole his hunting bow, he called the police, and I found recovery along the way. Some may think that this relationship could never be salvaged. But there he was, coming over all the time and clean out our fridge and pantry. He was a part of my life again, and providing a few snacks and dinners was worth having him around.

Brandon became a professional mixed martial arts competitor. His amateur career ended with an impressive 11-5 record after winning an amateur championship belt in 2014. Once someone goes "pro" in MMA, they cannot go back to "ammy"; amateur fighting is a way to perfect your skills, get used to the pressure, and find out if you like getting hit in the face.

For whatever reason, Brandon doesn't mind getting the shit kicked out of him.

Wanting to do well in the professional world of MMA, my brother asked me to be his manager. Here I was, standing face-to-face with the very same brother that had called the police on me for betraying him— and he was asking me for help. I concealed my excitement and emotions. I wanted to cry just from the thought of what was developing. Not much more than three years or so earlier, he was screaming at me through the phone for being a thief and a liar.

"Ok, let's get to work," I said, hiding my tears. I mean, come on, he is a fighter and can't have a pansy as a manager.

"Really?" he asked.

"You bet."

We talked about marketing, fight opportunities, training schedules, and much more. We had a lot of work to do. I had to contact the matchmaker, Bob, from the St. Louis MMA promotion organization. That group puts on events in St. Louis and Kansas City, Missouri area, and they knew Brandon from his tough and skillful reputation from amateur fights.

I called the matchmaker. The fight they offered for Brandon's professional debut was, according to Brandon, a match made in heaven. They offered him the chance to compete against a guy that went by the name "Pork." Brandon was stoked and didn't hesitate to say yes after consulting with his coaches.

"Hell yeah, I'll fight that dude," he said with a laugh. "It's already over."

"Got it," I said, "I'll let Bob know."

It was set. The contract was emailed to me, and I printed it off for Brandon to sign. We hit social media with the news and pictures to draw interest from friends, family, and fans.

Brandon "Quickdraw" Lowe went to work at his official eight-week training camp, and I got busy with promoting, marketing, and selling tickets. I was able to get him digital news coverage from a local media outlet, and we were generating a lot of interest in his professional debut match. Podcasts, phone interviews, news articles...we did it all.

He was training hard, tickets were selling fast, and the trash talk continued between the fans of each fighter.

Suddenly, three weeks before the fight, I got a phone call.

I could hear heavy breathing on the other end.

"Ty, dude, my back is hurting badly. What do you think it is?"

One thing I learned in recovery is not to react so brashly and abruptly. "What kind of pain is it? Pulled muscle, maybe?"

"Nah, I have never felt pain like this. It burns and seems to start in the back and travels to the front of my abdomen. It's weird."

"Have you tried sitting in the tub and soaking?"

"Not yet. I guess I will do that."

Inside I was worried. I wasn't sure what was going on, because Brandon is tough and hardly ever complains of pain. He had his nose broken once and was training the next day, so for him to call me with pain complaints was something that grabbed my attention.

I laid there, wondering what it could be. *Fingers crossed,* I thought.

Saturday afternoon came, and my phone rang again.

"Yep?"

More heavy breathing, now more like panting.

"Dude, this really hurts. I don't know what's going on? What do I DO!?"

I wasn't sure what to tell him except one thing. "I would go to the hospital and have them check you out."

"The hospital? I don't wanna go to no damn hospital. Ugh!"

"It's better to get it looked at than be in pain. Just don't let them give you a bunch of pain pills."

A few hours went by, and I had not heard from him. Getting nervous, I called his phone. No answer. I called his girlfriend's phone. No answer there, either. *Hmm...* I paced the living room floor.

Christina knew I worried. As a nurse, she saw me going into panic mode and did her best to calm me down. But it had now been four hours.

When his girlfriend called, she was talking to someone else in the background, and at first, I thought she had called me accidentally.

"HELLO! HELLO! ANYONE THERE?" I screamed.

There was some more chatter, then she finally answered. "Hello, oh, sorry. I was talking to the doctor."

"Yeah, what's going on?"

"He is getting ready to go back for surgery."

I was caught off guard.

"Surgery? What the hell do you mean, surgery? He fights in three weeks! What is wrong?"

"His appendix was on the verge of rupturing. He has appendicitis and has to have an emergency

100

appendectomy. He is distraught. Doc said he wouldn't be ready to fight in three weeks."

"Alright," I said, letting out a loud sigh. "Let me know how he is after surgery."

That evening, Brandon was crushed that he wasn't going to be able to have his professional debut in June. I have only heard my brother cry two times in my life. The day he called the police on me, and the day he knew his fight wouldn't happen.

I did my best to be a big brother by encouraging him that his professional debut would come soon. I told him something I heard at a recovery meeting - a small setback for a major comeback. He chuckled and seemed to be in better spirits by the time we hung up. It was at that moment that I felt like his big brother again - another example of my broken relationships being restored.

Summer came, and it was time for a yearly family reunion. We pulled up to the park, and I saw family (some I didn't even know) scattered around the pavilion. Kids were playing, while a few family members huddled around the food table, impatiently waiting to eat.

We got the kids out of the car and put the boys in their stroller. I happened to see my grandpa (my mom's dad) walking from his car, holding a white box.

I told Christina I needed to talk to him.

I was nervous. I hadn't talked to him since I'd gotten clean and sober. He was wearing a tucked-in, maroon button-up with blue jeans. He'd worked at Olin, a local ammunition manufacturer, for more than 30 years, and even after retirement, was sporting his black Winchester hat.

I cautiously approached him.

"Hey… uhm, Grandpa. I, uh, want to talk to you," I nearly murmured.

He stopped walking and scowled at me. "Uh-uh, not yet. I don't want to talk to you right now."

I didn't want to make him upset, so I obliged his request. "Okay."

I wasn't sure what to do. I stood there for a while. I'd tried to make amends with my grandfather, and he hadn't wanted to hear a peep from me. I waited awkwardly for him to make it to the pavilion with the pecan pie that was in the white box before I turned the other way, heading back to the car.

Christina tried asking me what was wrong. I just told her I would be right back.

I made my way to the car, opened the door, and sat down. I sat in silence and cried. My heart was heavy, and it was difficult to breathe. I wasn't crying because my grandfather didn't want to hear my apology. I cried because I was reminded of how badly I had hurt him. I wasn't just crying; I was sobbing. I remembered all of the times I had stolen from him and made him uncomfortable in his own home. A man that had worked his ass off for his family for more than 30 years had seen his trust misused and betrayed.

Eventually, I quit crying, dried my eyes, and returned to the pavilion where everyone was now eating. I talked, laughed, and caught glimpses of Grandpa doing the same. I knew that this wasn't the day for healing that relationship, but I understood more than ever how we could hurt the ones that love us.

Side note: It wasn't until later that year in December for Grandpa's birthday that I would be allowed to properly make amends.

For Grandpa's birthday, I sent my mom with a letter wishing him well and to tell him thank you for all the amazing things he had done for me over the years.

Grandpa read the letter and called to invite me over.

I arrived, and Grandpa and I talked privately where I was able to directly apologize for lying, stealing, and misusing his trust. He told me how proud of me he was, and we closed that moment with a hug. My grandpa is not a hugger.

Chapter 14
The Ongoing Fight to Victory

And, as is always the case, time goes on. The end of August came, and I was enrolled back in college, working toward a degree in communications with a minor in psychology. It was difficult getting back into school; I decided to go the online route through a university in Colorado (recommended by my friend, Jared).

A few days after aggravating homework – I was trying to get back into the swing of reading and writing papers – I got a call from the matchmaker for a potential fight for my brother, Brandon. This time, Brandon could be on the preliminary card for the second largest MMA promoter in the world at the Scottrade Center in St. Louis. This was HUGE! I told the matchmaker I would call him back.

I scrambled to dial Brandon's number.

"Hello?"

"DUDE!"

He laughed a little bit. "What?"

"So, I just got off the phone with Bob. You know Bellator is coming to town. He is offering you a fight on the prelim card for your pro debut."

"Really? Dang, who they want me to fight?"

I told him the name of the opponent, and suddenly a hush fell over the phone.

"They want me to fight *him* at 145 pounds?"

"Yep."

"I gotta talk with my coaches. I can beat him; I am just not sure I am ready for that yet. He's a tough dude."

Brandon had to play it smart. His professional fights would now have to be considered differently than his "ammy" career. This was an opportunity most do not get.

Eventually, he decided to take the fight. With a little over eight weeks for his training camp, his diet changed, and his training was more intense. He was in the *zone*; the last four weeks of his training, I would text him motivational quotes daily.

So many great moments took place so quickly. My family and I moved into a new, larger house for our growing family. Christina and I played on a co-ed softball team together, and the team was like family.

I purchased a ring, deciding it was time to ask Christina to be my wife.

We played a game that day, and I can't remember if we won or lost. I was so nervous about what she would say. Only a few people knew I was going to propose. My oldest daughter brought a few balloons that said congratulations (I was entirely against the balloons because there was a chance Christina could have told me to get bent).

We stepped off of the field and gathered our gear. Christina's mom, Beckie, brought me the ring as Christina was casually talking to a few of our teammates by the bleachers. I approached as her back was turned to me. I was getting ready to get on one knee like they do in the movies. I stood back up and looked over my shoulder at my kids sitting with Beckie, their grandmother, and our lifesaver. They were all smiling. Christina's dad, Mark, also knew what I was about to do.

I got on one knee. I grabbed Christina's hand as she turned around, looking confused.

"Uh... what are you doing?" she asked.

I turned my ball cap backward and looked her in the eyes, pulling out the black diamond engagement ring (Christina always said she would want a black diamond for a wedding band). She cocked her head and grinned. I started getting choked up.

"I know I am not perfect, but you make me want to pursue perfection. Will you marry me?"

I was able to see the team we played stand and wait in anticipation. I looked back over my shoulder and my oldest daughter, Dorie, was crying. I looked back up at Christina, and she was crying.

"Yes," she yelled. "YES!"

We were no longer boyfriend and girlfriend, but fiancés. We went home and celebrated.

Brandon's last week of training came. His weight wasn't where he wanted it to be - he was still over 160 pounds, which was 15 pounds heavier than his allowed weight. He was getting frustrated. He did everything he needed to cut weight, and aggravation and stress started attacking his focus.

Friday morning came. He had spent the night going through drastic measures to cut the weight needed. Beginning late Thursday morning, he and his training partner got busy, including the use of my jet tub, on the final weight cut. The first few hours he dropped almost eight pounds.

The seconds turned into minutes...with every second that passed, Brandon knew he couldn't miss weight for such a big night. We sold more than 120 tickets, and he didn't want to let everyone down.

He couldn't cut any more weight. He was nearly there, but it was time to head to Ballpark Village to check in and eventually attend the official weigh-ins that would be streaming live online. He put on his sweat suit and his training partner drove him to St. Louis.

Christina and I joined them later that evening, just minutes before his official weigh-in. The key players and promoters were standing on stage, as a few of Brandon's teammates eagerly watched. One foot on the scale. Then the next foot. *Shit!* He was over by a quarter of a pound. They brought out the blanket to shield Brandon as he took off his shorts to see where his weight was without the clothes. Still over. He was given one hour to make weight.

He slipped back into his sweat suit, but we made it only out of the rear entrance near where they were parked. Brandon's lips were chapped, and mouth was dry from his first weight-cut in more than a year. He fell to the ground as his muscles punished him for neglecting them. Cramps were happening all over his body. He screamed that he would just take a pay cut. His training partner encouraged him to get up and head to the truck to turn the heat on.

"We can do this, B," he said. "We have one hour to drop that quarter of a pound."

Brandon rolled on the ground in agony.

"One hour, Brandon, that is all you have. I support you either way," I said, cheering him on.

He took a sharp breath, and then stood up and walked to the truck. Christina and I waited patiently for 45 minutes. When they returned, we walked with them to the weigh-in room on the second floor of Ballpark Village. I had bottles of electrolyte fluids for him once he weighed in.

He stepped on the scale. Exactly 145 pounds. Brandon smiled from ear to ear. He ran off the scale and chugged the drink. He had lost 15 pounds in a little over 24 hours. That is either insanity or supreme dedication. Either way, he was on his way to his professional debut.

The next morning rolled around...fight day. I cannot tell you exactly what goes through the mind of a fighter the day of the fight, but it looked to me like a calm moment of reflection. Brandon had come a long way. Win or lose, he was still a champ in my book.

Four children, engaged, developing a not-for-profit, my mother living with us, talking with my father almost daily, and now as my brother's manager, I was about to see him through his professional debut on a grand scale.

He hung around our house for a little bit and left in the early afternoon for the check-in and photo shoot. Then it was our time to go, and I was nervous; I can only imagine how my brother felt. We drove to the arena, and I couldn't help but think about how far we had come as brothers...picking on each other, through my addiction, and now as fighter and manager.

We arrived at the Scottrade Center and found our seats. I looked around and saw so many people there to support Brandon. I sat in my chair, mesmerized by the size of the crowd. The first fight started, then the second, the third, and the fourth.

It was time for Brandon to enter the cage. You could hear everyone chatter about the fight about to happen. The lights dimmed, the music began playing, and out came his opponent. I waited and prayed he would be okay. Brandon had worked since he was fifteen to get to this moment. His song began playing, and we started hooting and hollering. Screams for my brother were loud, and it warmed my heart to see and hear those that stood behind him.

The ring announcer introduced the fighters and the corners they were in. Brandon danced on his toes, bouncing back and forth in anticipation. His opponent walked back and forth, staring. The bell rang. They touched gloves, and it was "go time."

Brandon checked a few kicks and threw a few jabs. They sized each other up. The opponent kept throwing leg kicks, which was to be expected. Brandon shot in for the takedown, and they wrestled around for position and control. Brandon had the opportunity to hook the leg, but he froze. He just stopped. We couldn't figure out what was going on. Then his opponent took his chance to capitalize on the mistake and dropped a huge elbow.

In a blink of an eye, it was over. My brother laid there, and we in the seats couldn't understand what had happened. I quickly grabbed my phone and texted the promoter. *We want another fight soon. That was not Brandon out there tonight. Thank you for the opportunity.*

I was worried about my brother. Not that he lost; remember, he is still a champ in my book. But I was worried how he would react. He'd put in weeks of daily training.

Maybe he wasn't ready yet.

I started questioning if I should have been more cautious about this fight. I held my wife's hand, waiting for Brandon to join us after the rest of the match-ups. The entire time I kept thinking to myself if he would be okay.

When I saw him, he was wearing a Bellator t-shirt the promoters had given him, and a few friends and fans huddled around him. You could hear him talking with everyone as he went over what he could have done differently. He was smiling, so that was a great thing.

I walked up to him to shake his hand.

"Sorry, I didn't win," he said, shaking his head in disbelief.

I hugged him. "Hey, don't apologize. You still won tonight. You got to see where you're at, fought a tough dude, and now we go up from here."

Someone I didn't know wanted a picture with Brandon. Then someone else wanted a picture. And another. He was surrounded by people telling him what a great job he had done. I could see his frustration melt away from the positive support.

Positive support makes all the difference in any situation.

It felt good, as a brother and a manager, to see him chase his dreams and work so hard. Through the experience of managing him, I had been able to witness what it takes to be determined and have a passion for success at something we love. I loved my recovery and was, and still am, willing to go to any length to hold onto it and grow through the process.

The night of my brother's professional debut, I learned that sometimes, during times of uncertainty, we learn the most valuable lessons that we can later use to help ourselves and others.

Thank you, Brandon "QuickDraw" Lowe; I have learned much from you.

Chapter 15
God Doing for Me What I Cannot Do for Myself

In the midst of everything else going on, I had the idea to write an autobiography.

I kept thinking to myself, *who in the actual hell would want to read about me?* I had been writing short stories for a while, mainly for practice, but still felt a lot of mechanics needed to be worked on. I went with the flow and started penning a story about my life, starting from the age of fifteen.

I blended my fiction flow with an autobiographic style. I revisited the streets of St. Louis and the memories of following dealers from one block to another before buying the heroin. I visualized what I went through and who I was with, and I activated parts of my brain that brought back the vivid memories of the chaos and personal hell in which I was once trapped. The memories were so real; I could even remember the smells of specific moments.

By November of 2015, my memoir was finished. I was excited and began looking for an editor, while my friend Mark began working on the cover art. We decided a death's-head hawkmoth would be a pretty cool addition and add appeal to the book, which now had a title - *Heroin Rising: A Tale of True Terror.*

Kevin, another lifelong friend, assisted me in formatting the text for paperback and digital once I got back the edited draft. We sat there for a few hours, reminiscing and poking fun at one another. He stayed with me through my addiction, spending hours talking to me and trying to convince me to get well.

I was continuing to go to 12-step meetings, and life was really pretty great. I couldn't believe how far I had come. I was still praying every morning and evening, and I was scheduling meeting after meeting as I networked with businesses and local leaders about the not-for-profit project. We began taking those in early recovery to various organizations that were in desperate need of volunteers.

Next, I tackled writing a play about addiction, family dynamics, and the stark and authentic message of a drug overdose. I wrote the original script in a three-day marathon writing session. I would get up at 4 in the morning and write for a few hours. After it was finished, I relied on social media to find a few professional (or at least inspired/inspiring) actors. I wasn't concerned about the level of experience; the message was in the dialogue, and I would hope the actors would bring it to life.

If I Never Wake Up was intended to have a one-time performance. Audra reached out to me, wanting to play one of the female characters, and a young gentleman (if this person is reading this, yes, I called you a gentleman, Jake) met me at a restaurant and agreed to play the antagonist, Christian.

It was coming together quite nicely. I was contacted by a friend whose daughter, Madison, was interested in playing the lead. The problem was the script. She requested to read it and was concerned with some of the dark and traumatic moments in the original version. This goes against my rules as a writer, but I said that I would modify the scenes and get her a new script. Something inside me told me to change it, so I listened to that feeling.

I sent her the revised version, I also found someone to play another character, Kara, but early vibes just weren't quite right. One evening during a family outing at a local restaurant, my cousin, Justin, said he would like to play the role of the father, and another cousin, Breann, expressed interest in the part of Kara if something opened up.

This was all coming together too easily.

One last thing to do – find a theater. Shouldn't be a problem, right? I left messages with several theaters, to no avail. I talked to a few others, and they declined to have us, or else the cost to rent their space was astronomical.

I was starting to get discouraged, and then I received a call from the actress set to play the mother, who told me she could no longer play the part. Ugh…

Wait! I thought. The actress playing Kara was not quite right, but she would fit nicely in the mother's part. My cousin stepped into the role of Kara, and just like that, the cast was set.

I called my last theater lead, fingers crossed. *I'm sorry, we can't help you...but...we do have a number to a woman who runs a theater in Granite City.*

I was thankful for their help, but I was not feeling very hopeful. I dialed the number I was given, and it felt like it rang forever.

When Brenda, the Executive Director of Alfresco Performing Arts Center, answered, I wasn't even 30 seconds into my pitch, and she said, "Yep, you can do it here."

I was caught off guard. "Uh… don't you wanna hear about the rest of the play?"

"It sounds like the kind of wonderful play that we need right now. Get in touch with my associate and you guys can coordinate a date."

She and I have been friends from that day forward.

The process moved very quickly. We scheduled the play for a month before the release of my autobiography, and we had an official table reading after the entire cast was selected. We gathered props and discussed the performance as a team.

The day came for our first stage rehearsal; we had Thursday night to Saturday morning to rehearse. An old friend I considered a big brother was visiting town and jumped on board, helping with stagehand duties and whatever else we needed.

I couldn't tell you how nervous I was. This was my first theater production as a playwright and director. Actually, this was my first production, ever. We had the first rehearsal with scripts in hand and made modifications as we went along. We removed a few props that seemed to just get in the way. We stripped the stage design for most of the scenes to only a table and three chairs; that allowed the dialogue and emotions to shine through to the audience.

The day of the performance, we went through it one more time, and then some of the cast and crew left for a few hours while I stayed behind. I sat in a seat that used to serve as a pew. I marveled at the beauty of the church, and couldn't help but think of how far we had come— me, my family, new and old friends. The quiet hum of silence filled the theater. Clean and sober, I couldn't help but revere at the blessings I had been given. I closed my eyes, sat up straight, placed each hand palm down on my knees, and prayed.

"God, whether You are a he, she, or just energy that was mine for the taking, I cannot thank you enough for what I have received in my life today. Please, bless all of the cast and crew and allow them to be safe. Please let those in the audience hear the message we bring to them tonight. I am not perfect, and I thank you for blessing me with the notion that I don't have to be. Amen."

Suddenly, it was six in the evening. The doors were going to be opening in thirty minutes, and I'd lost my script, again. I was padding around, mumbling obscenities under my breath. My stomach started to cramp. *No, no....this is not the time for that! Ugh*...and then I found my script and met everyone in the back, as my stomach settled.

A few people volunteered to be ushers and hand out programs at the door. We sat in the green room talking, laughing, and sharing funny moments from rehearsals. Five minutes before the curtain was set to rise, we all huddled together, where I thanked everyone for their hard work, and we said a prayer together.

A guest speaker introduced the evening, and then the lights dimmed. Suddenly, the audio of Aurora's birth played. After the audio stopped, you could hear the light coughs and murmurs from the crowd.

"Cue the lights, stage right," I directed in my headset.

"Aurora, we will call her Aurora," the mother said.

The father, arm around her, gazed upon their newborn daughter.

"Hi, my little miracle, my sugar bear," he calmly said.

Before we knew it, scene one was over. Scene two focuses on Aurora's life as a teenager. I was biting my nails, script in hand, hoping they didn't forget their lines. I had nothing to worry about...they nailed it.

The lights faded, the actors moved offstage, and we placed the dinner table and chairs center stage.

"Cue the lights," I instructed.

Oh my God! The next scene had already started when I realized that I had forgotten to place the brownies on the table. My heart started beating in panic. I didn't know what to do. I didn't want to run on stage and take the audience away from the moment. Madison, the actress playing Aurora, realized I forgot the brownies, and in superstar fashion, she worked around my gaffe, and the scene continued flawlessly. I let out a sigh of relief and smiled.

It was now time for one of the most crucial scenes of the play – the first overdose. Aurora stood at her dinner table, alone. She had cycled her way through different drugs and now found herself doing heroin on an almost daily basis. She snorted an invisible line and began to feel dizzy. She fell to the ground, and her parents entered the stage. Mom was distraught. Her daughter was on the ground unresponsive. Dad shouted for her to call 911 and started CPR. The fire department arrived and was able to revive Aurora with Narcan.

Momentum was building. I could hear the audience from behind the curtain as they sniffled and cried.

The next scene was ready. Aurora and her friends, Christian and Kara, sat at the dinner table as Aurora snorted two fake heroin caps. Her friends heedlessly talked to one another as Aurora overdosed again. Chaos filled the stage. The kids did not know what to do. Christian refused to call the police for fear of going to jail. Kara pleaded with him to save her friend.

"Aurora is blue, Christian, DO SOMETHING!"

Christian paced back and forth as his mind raced to find a reasonable and seemingly selfish solution. "We're outta here," he commanded, grabbing Kara's arm and exiting stage right.

The lights focused in on Aurora's lifeless body. You could hear so many in the crowd sobbing. Aurora remained on stage, dead and alone, for a full minute. Dad entered stage right, grabbed his daughter and called 911. A few minutes later, the same firefighter was back. Dad was frantically performing CPR...but this time, it was too late.

"I'm sorry, there's nothing I can do," the firefighter said.

A deep bellow left her father's mouth at that exact moment. The pain came, rushing him like a freight train, and plowed him in the chest. His daughter, the one he held and cared for as a baby, was gone.

By this time the audience was an absolute mess. The message had gotten through.

The final scene would only add to the somber feeling. A human being, a child, preparing to graduate high school, lost their life...like countless others had over the past few years. We took an intermission to set up the stage for the climax.

As we pulled the casket on stage, you could hear a few audience members' comments. We pulled the podium on stage. It was time. "Amazing Grace" filled the theater.

A few people attending the funeral paid their respect to the parents. After everyone sat down, the music slowly faded into the distance, the father gave his daughter's eulogy, and the audience lost it.

Then, everyone on stage froze. Aurora stepped out of the casket. She said her final goodbyes to her dad and apologized to her mom. Aurora (Madison) then turned and faced the audience, walking toward them. She sat with her legs crossed, center stage, and stared. "Lucid Dreams" moaned from the speakers. Mom unfroze and joined Aurora, holding her. Dad joined them next, then the rest of the cast followed. I came from backstage, and we all stood, facing the audience, hands joined together. Full of emotions, we bowed.

I looked up, and people were standing and clapping. The entire audience gave the cast and crew a much-deserved standing ovation for their dedication to bringing alive a theatrical performance that had more than just a message of "don't do drugs."

We packed up our gear, thinking that we would never do the play again.

Boy, were we wrong. Calls, texts, and messages on social media poured in over the next few weeks, saying how good the play was and asking when it would be playing again.

We would go on to finish three more performances.

Still riding the excitement from the play, the time came for the release of my book, *Heroin Rising: A Tale of True Terror,* and the obligatory book signing and release party. I was nervous about who would show, and I ordered 50 copies to sell.

I couldn't believe how many people showed up. Jack even traveled down to be part of the release. I anticipated only selling maybe 15 copies, but we sold out, with people still trying to get copies. I took their names and was sure to order more for them.

Social media posts rolled in, with people saying they couldn't put the book down and that they had read it in only a few hours. Many people sent me private messages, relaying how they never knew what addicts go through. One person even said they wished they could have helped more after they saw me in public once, weighing only 165 pounds (today, I weigh 240).

My goal had always been to tell my story so others that are not familiar with addiction could understand what addiction does to someone. God allowed me to live it, share it, and embrace everyone's understanding. Though the editor missed a few grammar and structure errors, the message was loud and clear.

After the release, something weird started happening. Media outlets began contacting me. Libraries were asking for book signings. Local organizations asked me to speak and share my journey. It was a different feeling at first - the idea that someone valued what I said. With this type of attention, I had to remain balanced and practice humility.

I am not that important. I kept praying to God to allow me the ability to continue with a message that needed to be heard, but not be blinded by the flare of articles and extra attention. I only wanted to share with my community that we can get well...whether that is drug or alcohol addiction or other maladies.

One article ran, and a few days later I received a call from a gentleman that works at the treatment facility I attended while in drug court. The new director, Brad, in the gentleman's department wanted to meet. He told me the new director was younger than the last and more ambitious and creative in their approach toward substance abuse disorders.

We eventually met at the Garden Gate Tea Room (owned by Brenda that runs the theater where we had the play). I walked into the cottage-style restaurant to find a seat for us, but they were already there.

The new director wasn't at all what I was expecting. I thought he would be some 50-year-old guy, but he was closer to 40. He kind of reminded me of Papa Joe, the Don of the Mafia Crime Family, from the film *Boondock Saints*. Rocco, or the Funny Man, visited Papa Joe and was asked to tell a joke in one very memorable scene. The more I thought about it, it kind of had the "mobster meeting" vibe.

Picture it. I get a call from a guy after seeing me in the paper. He tells me that his boss wants to meet. What? Is this boss of yours untouchable and keeps people at a distance? I walk into the restaurant, and they are already sitting there waiting for me. The restaurant is dimly lit, and they are sitting in the corner with their backs to the wall so they can see everything in front of them.

As long as he doesn't ask me to tell a joke, we are good.

He stood up from the table and introduced himself.

"Hi, my name is Brad. Thanks for meeting us today."

We sat down and discussed the menu. I had eaten there a few times before, and they asked what I recommended, which was what they wound up ordering. We joked and laughed, but mostly we talked about Amare and what direction we were going with the community. Brad wanted to partner on a few volunteer projects we were doing by allowing current drug court clients to get out and give back.

Okay, so maybe this wasn't the mob, after all.

We decided to work together on volunteering efforts so that clients that were interested could come volunteer with us. I left the tea room that day, completely overwhelmed with gratitude. This moment would be the first of many revolutionary changes still to come. God was doing for me what I couldn't do for myself, and I was excited to see where we were going to go next.

Chapter 16
I Do

One of the most significant gifts that I received in finding recovery was the shift in my perception.

I realized that I was the maker of most of my own suffering. This is what I mean...let's say I want a new truck. The truck is my motivation to work hard. If this truck is $30,000 and requires me to put down $4,000 to finance, well now I have a short-term goal of the down payment. I work nearly every day to make money to save for this truck. The salesman would advise me that to afford my goal of a $300 a month car payment, I would have to enter a seven-year loan. The interest I would end up paying, in the end, would be quite hefty.

Halfway through saving for the down payment (I have about $3,000 saved), let's say I lose my job. All I can think about is the truck I am not going to be able to get. I assume I would desperately look for another job, but it seems that no one is hiring. I submit application after application. No callbacks. I have now hit a crucial point where I have to start dipping into my savings for the down payment.

After a few weeks, I have had two job interviews and $300 left in my savings. I ponder life. I don't understand why things happen to me. I am a good guy. I just want this truck. Why won't anyone hire me? I am never going to have this truck. My posture slouches. My motivation starts to sink because the job I was able to get only allows me to make enough to cover my bills. The truck I wanted will never be mine.

Screw the truck. The truck only served as a meaningless point of motivation. I had to ask myself in early recovery what truly motivated me outside of a materialistic agenda. Becoming healthier, kinder, and reliable is what drove me. I set out to achieve it. I built a routine. I started getting up every day at four in the morning. I worked hard. I eliminated excuses. I learned to evaluate where I was.

The strange thing is, since I fell to my knees on August 19, 2012, I have not had a bad day. To have a bad day, one must close their eyes and go to sleep with negative *shit* on their mind. The negative *shit* in my mind is only *shit* that bothers me and maybe a few other people. We all have different motivation and mental models. We all want respect, but few of us want to give it. We crave the sun and spit at the moon. The world just is. I don't control the outcome; I manage the decisions I make. I learned to pray for acceptance of the outcome (result). I also learned *shit* makes a great fertilizer; I began using negative thoughts to find the positive.

Metanoia. Aha moments. Epiphany. Revolution of the heart and mind. The shift in my perception of how and why this world works the way that it does was being laid out in front of me. So many people were shouting at one another. Human beings hurting one another, whether through physical violence, the stroke of a pen, or the words from their tongue was apparent. It was what frightened me as a child. I couldn't wrap my mind around the ignorance we transmit daily. But, my "aha" moment came from working towards a goal that was driven by a motivation to do better - motivation to stop wanting so much and wanting to give so much more.

I was my own worst enemy; I understand that phrase today.

I understand that as a collective society if you take a thousand people who have no idea what they are doing and just want to complain and trample each other to the top by any means necessary, you have a society that will eventually implode in on itself. We have senators, governors, presidents, bosses, wardens, CEOs, mothers, fathers, creditors...the list can go on, but all of these individuals seek control in some form and fashion. We are born into a world that hungers for control, and you had best believe that someone will yield that over you and me.

I found that turning my will over to a power of paramount proportions has made all the difference in my overall happiness. I now found a way; what positive psychology calls flourishing. Buddhism speaks of lessening our suffering. Taoism talks about finding balance and accepting what is. The way I found to do this above all else was to pray in the morning and evening (and maybe even a few times during the day).

I learned that strengthening my connection with a power greater than me has opened the floodgates of understanding. Through this process, I no longer wanted to *"fight anyone or anything."* One person I learned to quit fighting was myself. Some of you reading this will understand what I am about to say - I ultimately felt I was 'in the fourth dimension.' The here and now is what counted. My decisions yesterday affected me at this exact moment. I lived a life that was bent on using my five senses to find tangible proof of my being. I developed a sixth sense, a presence that gives me goosebumps when I listen - the moment of assurance that things will be okay.

The master plan isn't really a plan at all. It is what I am willing to do with the power that is given to me. I can take power from a job, from money, from holding a gun and telling prisoners to do as I say and use it to cause destruction and madness. Or, I can take a power that is floating in front of my face, unseen to the naked eye, and grab and harness it for bettering my life and the lives of those around me.

I was once told that we are spiritual beings, having a human experience. Positive and negative energy are of the same force. Cut from the same cloth. To me, it seems that it is always about power. It would make sense why my life became so powerless and unmanageable. This can happen to someone that is not an addict. In my powerlessness, I caused a lot of destruction, which leads me to believe that I did harness power but did not know how to use it effectively.

There has been a lot that has transpired over the course of my five years of recovery...sobriety...clean time...whatever you would like to call it. I learned to cherish the moments given to me.

For those of you that have children, have you ever sat and watched them eat? Have you ever paid attention while they watched cartoons and smiled, awed with the definition of their facial structure, the sound of their laugh, the color of their hair, and the way their body moves? I watch my children and think back to the day they were conceived. And, no, I don't know the exact day, but I think of how two gametes meet for the first time, and at that moment, they form a relationship that becomes life—a life that I have been given to protect, cherish, and admire.

Since I met Brad from the treatment facility, he offered me a job for a position that was made possible by a grant. I went back to where I received treatment and worked with current drug court clients. Man, you should have seen their eyes the day I introduced myself to the drug court clients in group. I could see some eyes flicker with the hope that they, too, can escape their madness.

Shortly after becoming employed with the treatment facility, Christina's wedding came. I say her wedding because it was all about her. She tolerated me for years, running in and out of her and our daughters' lives. She sat up late at night, wondering if I was going to overdose and die when no one had heard from me for days. She looked in her wallet to see that I had stolen her gas money to get to work. She is the one that watched me sleep as my breathing was almost non-existent. She is the one that fought with our oldest daughter to get dressed in the morning while I was sleeping on someone's couch or bed. She was the one that was neglected when all she wanted was for me to be part of her family. She was the one that had to cry into the phone with one of her best friends when I weighed 165 pounds and lost my mind. She was the one that answered the phone and stomached talking to me while I sat in the psych ward after trying to harm myself. She was the one that bought me a few new clothes so I could at least try to feel a little better about myself.

She was the one that laid in bed at night, wondering if I was even worth it.

So, this wedding was her day. I stood and watched the groomsmen put on their red chucks she wanted us to wear. Everyone was laughing and joking. My best friend, Justin, gave me a hard time, as I would expect him to. My brother stood there as both a man and a best friend...the one that helped save my life. Christina's cousin Kenny stood tall and smiled for this day.

Christina deserved all of this.

I couldn't help but think about the people that, more than five years ago, had said she should have given up on me, that I would never change. Many people turned their back on me. They had to; I had turned my back on myself.

I have since learned that when we are ready to change, we will go to any length to change. When we have had enough of the madness is when we will search for an everlasting meaning that, as I stated before, allows us to reach the fourth dimension. No real progress comes about without change anyhow.

Many small moments led to this grand moment. The pastor that was marrying us had me come to the stage. People packed the seats to see Christina's big day. My mother, Doreen, looked beautiful. My soon to be mother-in-law, Beckie, looked beautiful. I stood on the stage watching everyone. I already had tears trying to escape, and the music had not even started yet.

Everyone was seated, and the music played. My children were there. My family and friends were there. And I was *there*. I wasn't drunk, high, in jail, or in treatment. Kenny stood by a picture of Christina's late sister, Julie. Before we started the ceremony, he told me that if I hear him say "hairy balls" on stage, not to think he had gone bonkers. I laughed it off, but we stood on stage before Christina joined us, and I understood what he meant.

He took a piece of paper out of his pocket. Under his breath, he said, "Hairy balls, hairy balls, hairy balls, hairy balls, hairy balls, hairy balls, hairy balls..."

I wanted to laugh but controlled myself. Kenny is a pretty funny guy, and he was taking a comedic approach to holding his composure. He was getting ready to give a speech about Julie, who everyone had loved so much. Julie lost her life in a tragic car accident many years before.

He read his piece of paper as best that he could. His voiced cracked, the tears fell, and Julie, in a way, was able to join us for the day.

And then, it was the moment everyone was waiting for. Christina, the most beautiful and stunning bride, would be walking down the aisle. I looked around the room, and a soothing layer of peace lilted down onto the crowd.

The doors lightly creaked open. Christina and her father stepped over the threshold. It felt like someone punched me in the gut when I laid my eyes on her for the first time in her dress. The white shrouded her in a lovely way; it clung to her body perfectly, highlighting each curve with perfection. I had never seen anything so perfect and sexy. If I remember correctly, the pastor had to close my open mouth from astonishment (I could be making this part up).

Her father passed her to me to protect, hold, and care for. I was nervous that I wouldn't be the man she needed me to be. I had so many thoughts running through my head when she stepped on that stage.

Christina was given the opportunity to say her vows. Then it was my turn. I tried to memorize them, but I had to pull out my notes. I unfolded the paper and took a deep breath. I looked at Christina and was mesmerized by the beauty that stood before me. If I ever have felt blessed in my life, this was one of those moments. I cleared my throat and read what I had written.

'When it rains, it pours' is a saying we are both familiar with. A beautiful sunny day can suddenly be filled with a light rain turning into a violent thunderstorm. 'Batten down the hatches,' the captain will sometimes say on a ship when this unexpected storm approaches.

When we met one another, it started off as a beautiful sunny day. Then, one day, we felt our first light rain; we were able to pull through. Then, experiencing a few more sunny days, an unexpected storm was brewing on the horizon. It was a storm you were not adequately prepared to handle. You were told to abandon ship many times, but you refused. You stayed by my side, offering to steer us to safety many times. Until the rain and winds were too high, you had no choice but to save yourself.

A ship lost at sea I was. You came back to mend any holes and remove any waters that were weighing me down. At the time, I was a ship not worth salvaging, but you saw the potential. You somehow saw that I might have some worth and could sail again.

It may be difficult at times to ride the storms we will face, but our love knows no cowardice. Our love knows no limits; our love knows each other. As faced with adversities over the years, I did not deserve to be loved so kindly, as I loved so selfishly.

I swear never to abandon ship, no matter how turbulent the waters may become. I will stay positioned at the helm of the vessel with strength, courage, and love, embracing and protecting you for who you are – my wife. I swear to defend you and be your fearless captain whenever things get tough. And if that helm gets ripped from my hands, I will wrap my arms around you to give you the warmth and security you gave me in my time of need. When it rains, Christina, I will forever be there when it pours.

The pastor asked Christina, "Do you take this man to be your lawful wedded husband, to have and to hold from this day forward, for better, for worse, for richer, for poorer, in sickness and health, until death do you part?"

She gripped my hands tighter as we stared into each other's eyes. "I do."

"And, Ty, do you take this woman to be your lawful wedded wife, to have and to hold from this day forward, for better, for worse, for richer, for poorer, in sickness and health, until death do you part?"

Christina smiled at me. This was one of our biggest moments. I could run away as I did with everything else, or I could honor and assist my wife for the rest of our days. I admired her at that moment. I believe she was getting nervous because I was taking so long to answer.

My voice cracked, but I managed to say, "I do."

"I now pronounce you Mr. and Mrs. Bechel. You may kiss the bride!"

I grabbed my wife by her cheeks and pressed my lips softly against hers. The room disappeared, and time stood still. Suddenly, it was just the two of us. The electrifying moment was sealed when my slightly open and gentle mouth kiss lasted for about fifteen seconds.

I could hear those attending hoot and holler, whistle, and clap for our big day.

As I stepped off the stage, I couldn't believe I was married.

Holy shit, I am married!

We left to take pictures and soon joined everyone at the reception. So many people came and joined us; I have no words for what I felt. The feeling is, well, indescribable.

I just…I don't know where I would be today without Christina and so many others. I decided to turn my will and life over to the care of a God that I understood and have taken action (and more action) to become a better person every day since.

I now had the prettiest wife in all the universe. What next?

Chapter 17
86,400

Thank you, thank you, and thank you for the time you have given to read this so far. I have learned that I am not that special or unique, and that is okay. I spent many years trying to be something I am not. Today, I can be happy with who I am and excited for what is to come.

I stared at this blank page, wondering what I should write. I was one chapter away from finishing. I had no choice but to go back through my life and think about everything I have been able to experience. In five years of recovery, I have been blessed with a wife, healthy children, so many great friends (A.J. G., Kim C. (GUCCI), AJ F., Liz B., Darryl P., Frank S., Justin B., Chris K., Tammy I., and so many more), a job, an opportunity to help build a not-for-profit (Amare) with a fantastic Board of Directors, education, and love. The list of blessings could go on for page after page.

I GET to experience life to the fullest today. I spent so much time thinking I had to always be *happy*. Happy isn't a state of feeling "good" all the time. I have learned a lot from my sadness and adversities; I have learned every second can offer knowledge that I didn't have the second before.

I am a bag of flesh and bones, and inside me is an energy that will leave once this shell ceases to pump life.

Where my energy goes upon death is beyond me, and that is okay. I have taken an idea that Hell on Earth is real, but that Hell is forged in the mind I possess and the anchors I hold onto.

I am no longer afraid of death – Memento Mori. And, *I am no longer afraid to live and experience life to its fullest and all the blessings and pangs that come with it* – Memento Vivere.

I don't have control over much in this world, and I finally let go of the idea of being power hungry. I was hungry for something but couldn't quite figure it out at first. The drugs and alcohol were merely junk food that gave me no real nutritional value. They were distractions from the more significant, organic source of power. The hole I tried to fill up each second of the day was not able to be filled with the worldly distractions I desperately desired. That all changed on August 19, 2012. I continue to pray daily to assist in keeping me clean and sober one day at a time - thy will not mine. Helping people has proven a massive success in my life...and many others. I cannot find myself telling others honestly what to believe, but I do know something of the almost supernatural happened on that unforgettable day in August.

Finding a God to look up to kind of reminds me of the *I wanna be like Mike* slogan from the 1990s. So many kids wanted to be like Michael Jordan. They would watch, fantasize, idolize, and for some, they would work very hard to emulate the talent and success Jordan had. They bought his shoes, spent hours on the basketball courts, and even stuck their tongue out as he did. Today, I want to be better for everyone with whom I come in contact. That isn't always easy. The treatment facility I work at is full of many beautiful, magical, smart, and wonderful human beings that need a little guidance and will be able to achieve great things in their life once they decide to do something different.

I have learned so much from them, and I must thank them.

I have an idea that God is a force (energy if you must) that wants me to quit being ignorant toward people and myself. We can have hours upon hours of discussion about consequentialism (e.g., ethical egoism, social contract theory, utilitarian theory). We can discuss polytheism versus monotheism versus atheism (keyword - discussion - not an argument, trying to match wits and be more superior in knowledge than each other). We can get in the battle of "my dad can beat up your dad" discussion. I do believe we shouldn't be killing, stealing, and purposely trying to hurt one another. We can even discuss the non-consequential ethical theories, but all in all, the time spent with one another discussing differentiating ideas is a process I would cherish. I get to spend time with another human being that thinks differently than me, or even like me, and that, I believe, is the blessing. Realistic peace is something obtainable – JFK from June 10th, 1963 taught me that (Where we go one, we go all).

I learned there is not much progress without change, and change is a constant in the universe. So, yeah, I know many people on social media (and other places) say negative things about addicts, and you know what? That is okay. Most of us have said something horrible about someone (or even a group of people). We get kind of lost in what we think we know, which is usually wrong and led by some instinctual or psychological need to find somewhere to belong. Most of the time we just don't understand one another. Work with someone battling addiction that has battled trauma, heavy guilt/depression, and/or abandonment, many people would change their mind about addiction. Most people are not monsters.

Pick your position, some of us are told. Pick a side, a family member will say. Vote for your candidate on this here ballot. Which team do you like? Team Jacob or Team Edward? I am laughing at that last question. (By the way, since we are being honest, I was Team Edward. I love werewolves and all, but vampires are just a bit more mysterious and compelling).

I will continue to move forward in life - a second at a time, building more symbiotic relationships. There are symbiotic relationships all around us; think of the relationship we have with trees that allow us oxygen to breathe. I have learned so many things I have never known and had to unlearn things I was so arrogant about holding onto. I ended *Heroin Rising: A Tale of True Terror* talking about Mitakuye Oyasin (All Relations). It is a Lakota Indian prayer.

It is translated, "We are all connected." That prayer belongs to the Lakota Tribe and is beautiful, and I still use it as a frequent reminder.

You have 86,400 seconds in your day today. How are you going to use them?

Love,

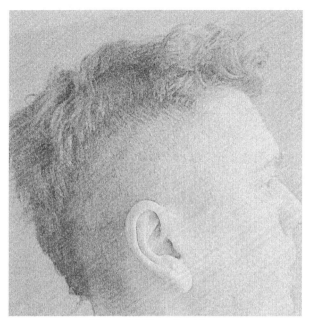

About The Author

T.A. Bechel, an Illinois native, is a writer of fiction, consisting of horror and thriller books.

Made in the USA
Columbia, SC
27 August 2018